ARMS OF THE SEA
Our Vital Estuaries

What is an estuary? It is the mouth of a tidal river, an arm of the sea, where the mingling of sea water with fresh provides a delicate balance essential to life. It supports plants basic to marine food chains, is a breeding ground and nursery for fish and wildlife, a natural flood-control system, a safeguard against silt for harbors and channels, and a precious recreational facility.

In superb nature writing, Elizabeth Shepherd chronicles the life cycle of the fish, the birds, the invertebrates and mammals whose existence depends on estuaries, and vividly communicates the urgent need for their preservation. Photographs of striking beauty show nature at its loveliest, while others show how man destroys it—at his peril.

Lothrop, Lee & Shepard Co./New York

Elizabeth Shepherd
ARMS OF THE SEA
Our Vital Estuaries

ILLUSTRATED WITH PHOTOGRAPHS

Other books by Elizabeth Shepherd

Tracks Between the Tides
Jellyfishes

TITLE PAGE PHOTOGRAPH:
The sea swells slowly up Shark River in the Everglades.

Shepherd, Elizabeth.
  Arms of the sea.

  SUMMARY: Describes the characteristics of estuaries and the life cycles of the various fish, birds, mammals, and invertebrates that depend on them.
  1. Estuarine ecology — Juvenile literature.
[1. Estuarine ecology. 2. Ecology] I. Title.
QH541.5.E8S54   574.5'2636   73-4951
ISBN 0-688-41558-X
ISBN 0-688-51558-4 (lib. bdg.)

1 2 3 4 5 77 76 75 74 73

Acknowledgments

For permission to reproduce the photographs which appear on the pages noted, I should like to thank the following organizations and individuals:

The United States Department of Commerce, National Marine Fisheries Service: 71, 100, 112, 150, 151, 152. National Oceanic and Atmospheric Administration: 76.

The United States Department of the Interior, Bureau of Sport Fisheries and Wildlife: 1, 10, 15, 42, 55, 65, 67, 107, 109, 114, 133; and especially Mr. Kirke A. King of the Gulf Coastal Zone Refuges: 75, 80; the National Park Service: 2-3, 22, 30, 34, 38, 57, 68, 79, 85, 88, 101, 142, 143, 153; the United States Geological Survey: 32, 135. The photograph on page 32, which also appears on the front cover, is by Aero Service, Litton Industries.

Those on pages 94, 97, 106, 137, 147 are U.S. Army Corps of Engineers Photographs, while those on pages 126 and 129 appear by courtesy of the American Museum of Natural History.

Credit for the back cover photograph, which is also reproduced on page 51, and for the photograph on page 37 goes to Gordon S. Smith of the National Audubon Society. Also from the National Audubon Society is the photograph on page 91 by Allan D. Cruickshank.

The photograph on page 120, as well as the one on page 63, was taken by Charles Marden Fitch, with special thanks to Christopher Quinn.

I should also like to thank Olga Marshall for her beautiful drawing of the food pyramid on page 82, and Thomas Feagans, Jr., for redrawing the diagrams on pages 56, 69, and 131.

The diagrams in this book are based upon material drawn from the following publications and organizations:

The National Estuarine Pollution Study. Washington, D.C. U.S. Government Printing Office, 1970, for 21, 23, 28, and 61.

The Conservationist and the New York State Department of Environmental Conservation, 46, 48, 56, and 69.

L. Eugene Cronin and A. J. Mansueti, "The Biology of the Estuary," in *A Symposium on Biological Significance of Estuaries*. Washington, D.C.: Sport Fishing Institute, 1971, 73 and 74.

Institute of Ecology, *Man in the Living Environment*. Madison: University of Wisconsin Press, 1970, 131.

George Vasey, *The Agricultural Grasses and Forage Plants*. Washington, D.C.: U. S. Government Printing Office, 1889.

The Washington State Department of Fisheries for the salmon cycle diagram, page 17.

I should also like to thank Joseph Dowhan, plant ecologist for the Fire Island National Seashore, who showed me the usefulness of transect studies, and A. S. Taormina, of the New York State Department of Environmental Conservation, for reading the galley proofs.

E. S.
Water Island, N.Y.

Contents

For Peter, Ann, and Adam

Salmon jump waterfalls and navigate other hazards, both natural and man-made, on journey upriver to spawn.

1

Salmon Going Home

With powerful thrusts of her tail, the salmon pressed on. Across the Pacific, northward and eastward she swam and, for hours at a time, she rested. She rested deep in the ocean, moving her fins just enough to stay in place.

A school of herring flashed by above her head. Her eyes followed them, but she did not pursue them. Fully grown now, her eggs slowly ripening, she had lost any desire to feed. Another and stronger urge drove her. It was time to spawn, to shed her eggs and start the next generation of salmon on its way.

Day after day the salmon went on. The hours of daylight grew longer, lengthening into summer. The vast cold waters she had roamed for the past two or three years were behind her. This year she was heading inland to the stream where she was born.

All around her were other salmon of her own age—females blue-gray like herself, males in red mating splendor—moving together in a large school. The

11

smells, the movements, the very presence of the other fish increased her desire to reach home.

The school could no longer ride the ocean currents. It had to work against them. Time and again, the female salmon found herself separated from the others, and struggled to rejoin them.

Sometimes great shadows darkened the water above her head—sea birds waiting their chance. The female salmon drew closer to the other fish, her body almost touching the ones nearest. For more safety, the school moved down into deeper water. When the sun was lower in the sky, they swam up again.

At last the odor of land, of home, reached them. The female salmon nipped the fish just ahead of her, as though to make him hurry. The shore was still distant.

All the next day the school pushed on. Heads and back fins surged into the air, making the water bubble and foam about the salmon. The odors of land became intense, overwhelming the fish's need for rest.

Bucking a current that ran along the shore, the female salmon found the opening she sought. The water, receiving rain and melting snow from the land, clearly had the smell of home. The sea shouldered its way in among the rocks and thrust an arm into the river mouth. Geographers call such openings "estuaries." The term comes from an ancient Sanscrit word, *aidh*, which meant "surge" or "swell."

The salmon rode the surging tide up the arm, up toward the land. Inside, she circled around and then drove deep down beyond pull of river currents and tide. Here her body, dragging with the weight of her eggs, could rest.

This meeting place of river and sea, this estuary, was but a way station on her long journey home. She still had hundreds of miles to go. But here where the waters were cool and deep, calmer than the sea, she stopped for a while.

This gave her time to adjust to the change of water. For inside the estuary the water was less salty than the open sea. It was of course diluted by the fresh river water, which drained the land.

As the river met the sea, it brought smells of the inland streams and brooks where salmon spawn. So even as the salmon rested, she kept sniffing, sniffing. Among all the odors, she detected some familiar ones.

The female salmon smelled birch trees, whose dead leaves fell into the stream where she was born. She smelled gravel and soil from the bottom where she had hidden as a tiny fryling. She smelled sawdust from a lumbermill she had passed as a young smolt headed for the sea. The river carried many other odors. Like buoys drawn on a chart, they marked her way. She could wait no longer.

Putting the salt sea behind her forever, she swam landward. For many weeks she swam. The river broadened out across low, muddy banks, gathering in many smaller streams that twisted through the land. And at last from one of these twisting streams she caught the special combination of smells that guided her home.

13

The stream branched, and the school broke apart, some fish going one way, the rest, like the female salmon, going the other. The water was shaded by tall spruce trees. Its coolness and the sense of home gave her new vigor. Her weary body moved more easily, more rapidly in the quiet water.

Suddenly the water became dangerously shallow. Just ahead, the stream was blocked by a long mound of earth heaped there by people in the nearby village.

Confused, the salmon circled around, trying to get into position for a leap. All her senses were tuned to the barrier, to the press of the water. She steadied herself with her side fins. Then, with a mighty burst, she leaped at the wall. The hard mud slapped her belly. Stunned, she fell back. She circled around again and leaped straight up, holding her side fins out.

Again she fell. The water was too shallow for her to gain the thrust she needed to clear the wall. And all about her, other salmon too were thudding against the wall, falling back. Overhead a hawk wheeled lazily about in the sun, watching.

Once more the female salmon leaped. This time she fell on the muddy bank. She lay still, mouth open, gills gaping. Her fins were ragged as though some crab had nibbled on them. Her skin was torn and dull.

She pushed her tail against the stream's soft bank. She had not eaten for a long time now, and her reserves of fat were almost gone. She flopped a little closer to the water. Flies buzzed over the mud.

The hawk dropped closer, and then soared upward.

Birds and bears hunt migrating salmon in Kamishak Bay, Alaska. As forests are cut down and logs shipped away, a once important source of nutrients is lost. Fortunately, salmon remains still supply minerals needed by plant life.

Drawing all her strength, the female salmon flopped over. The water lapped against her belly but she did not feel it. She lay still.

Soon her body would break down and become part of the soil, part of the stream. In the spring when young salmon hatched in the nearby brook, they would know her smell with the other stream smells. Much later, returning from the sea, they would follow the remembered smells, they too on their last journey, their journey upriver to spawn.

15

Though the dead salmon was a sockeye (*Oncorhynchus nerka*), the story is much the same for all the Pacific salmon, from small coho to mighty chinook weighing 100 pounds or more. Atlantic salmon (*Salmo salar*) are different. Their runs are shorter, so many can survive the spawning migrations and return a second or third time to spawn. Or at least once they could. Heavily fished, and barred from many streams by lumbering and other projects, the Atlantic salmon may now be almost extinct.

Other kinds of fish also make spawning migrations from sea to land. Among them are herring, striped bass, and sturgeon. Eels make the journey in reverse, spawning in the sea and growing up in fresh or brackish (partly fresh) water. Many crustaceans, such as crabs and shrimp, also follow this pattern.

Migrating sea animals can make the change from fresh water to sea water and from sea water to fresh water—a change that would kill other sea animals. Within limits, of course, a sea worm or a saltwater minnow can adjust to gradual changes in salinity, or saltiness. Heavy rains greatly freshen the water inside an estuary, while a long drought may leave it unusually salty. But if you drop a saltwater animal into fresh water or put freshwater worms or fish into salt water, the animal will die within minutes.

It was probably during the ice ages that migrating fishes developed their ability to adjust to such change. Scientists think that bony fishes such as salmon started life in fresh or partly fresh water several hundred mil-

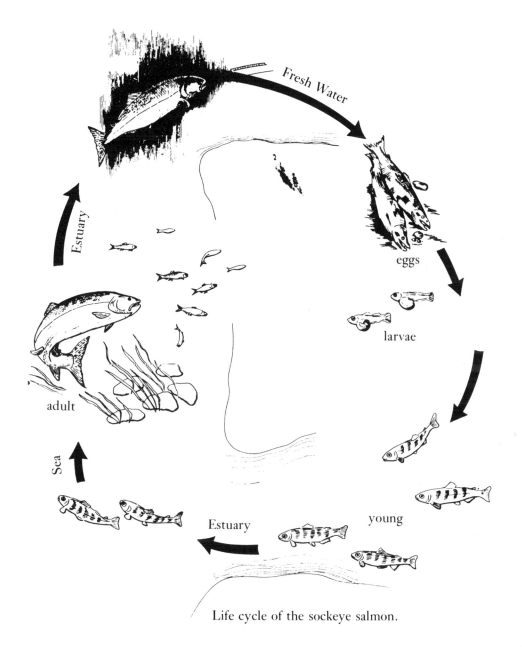

Fresh Water

Estuary

eggs

larvae

adult

Sea

young

Estuary

Life cycle of the sockeye salmon.

lion years ago. The fishes lived, spawned, and died in fresh water. Then, as melting ice freshened the northern seas, the fishes went ever farther into the sea to feed. To spawn, however, they returned to the inland

17

streams whose conditions were better for tiny young fry. Besides, their eggs apparently could not survive in salt water any more than they can today.

Many migrating fishes such as sturgeon and Atlantic salmon still remain close to shore. Striped bass raised in commercial hatcheries survive very well in fresh-water lakes. With adequate food supplies, they are able to live and grow up entirely in fresh water.

With those that still go to sea, the young fish do not plunge from their home rivers directly into the sea. Young sockeyes, for example, spend two weeks or more inside the river mouth where the waters are salty, but not as salty as the sea. Returning as adults, the salmon again spend a few days in the brackish water before running upriver. As the fish moves farther from the sea, the water becomes fresher and fresher. At last the salmon swims in water as sweet and fresh as rain.

As transition zones between land and sea, estuaries are way stations for migrating fishes. They are nurseries for their young and permanent homes for many other creatures. Almost all the fish and crabs and clams we eat depend on them at some stage of development.

Arms of the sea are nurseries and homes and way stations because they are traps, though traps of a very special sort. Most traps catch substances large enough for you to see and hold, while smaller things escape. In an estuary, the situation is reversed. The trap cannot hold a salmon or an eel—at least not for long. It can catch very tiny substances that nourish living beings, and that call the salmon home from the sea.

2

Trapped Between River and Sea

To a salmon, each arm of the sea has its own particular combination of smells, which together signal home. This may come from dead salmon and live salmon eggs, from wet bear fur, spruce needles, poplar bark, pebbles scoured from mountain rocks, soil washed off the land, chemical wastes from factories—from all sorts of bits and pieces of things.

These particles from living plants and animals, and from never living rocks and minerals, are carried downstream by rivers and trapped by the incoming tide. Some particles escape and are carried out to sea. For the most part, though, the particles are swirled around and around inside the arm, caught between tides and river currents.

No one would recognize these bits and pieces as tooth or leaf or pebble. Broken apart, ground down, decayed, only their basic substance is left, in the form of chemical compounds such as proteins, minerals, vitamins, and carbohydrates. Dissolved or suspended in the water, these compounds nourish many small sea

19

plants and animals. For this reason they are called "nutrients," and the arm of the sea that holds them is a "nutrient trap."

Sea tides, river currents, winds, waves, the sun itself, all trigger the nutrient trap. In the main, though, the tide is more important than any other single force. This is partly due to the nature of sea water. With about 35 parts of salt for every thousand parts of water, it is denser than fresh water. So as the tide moves into the mouth of a river, it does not rush against the fresh water with a tremendous splash. There may be much churning and foaming. Salt spray is flung into the air, air is stirred into the water. But fresh and salt water are not completely mixed from top to bottom.

Rather, the incoming tide tends to flow inland like a wedge under the fresh river water. The river water, being less dense, floats on top. The salt water mixes with the fresh water along the edge where they meet. The faster the tide flows, the more the water mixes along this edge, or "interface."

When the tide ebbs seaward, both layers flow in the same direction. Then the bottommost layers of salt water rise and replace the outrushing water. Thus the water keeps moving in a definite circular pattern: in and under, out and up.

This circular motion traps the nutrients inside the arm. For simplicity's sake, imagine some calcium compounds from the salmon's backbone. Swirled downriver, the compounds slowly sink, being heavier than the water. As they sink, they are caught by the incom-

20

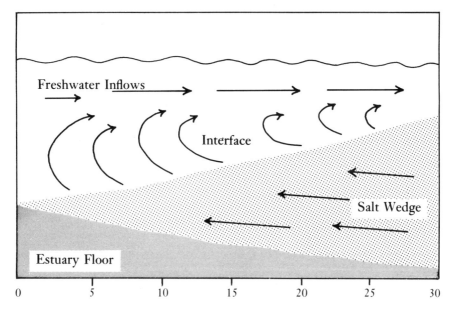

Freshwater Inflows

Interface

Salt Wedge

Estuary Floor

| 0 | 5 | 10 | 15 | 20 | 25 | 30 |

Salinity in parts of salt per thousand parts of water

Typical saltwater circulation pattern.

ing tide and driven inland again. They may be dropped on mud flat or wetland, or they may be flushed out toward the sea. Then, sifting to the bottom, they may once again be whirled upward and inland with bottom currents.

As the calcium compounds are moved around, some are soaked up by plants, some swallowed by clams or shrimplike organisms. So the nutrients are again trapped, this time in living beings. Eventually they may become part of a salmon or bear. And when the fish or mammal dies, of course the story continues. Nutrients are circulated and recirculated within the arm.

With any trap, the shape determines the way it

21

In Glacier Bay, Alaska, as elsewhere in the far north and on high mountain ranges, rivers of ice still flow seaward, chilling deep inlets and bays with their melt water.

works. If you look at a map of our continent, it is obvious that no two openings in the coast have exactly the same shape. Cook Inlet (Alaska), more than most, looks like an arm with its elbow bent against the mountains. Its fingers reach into the rivers that drain the glacier-topped mountains. Because the "shoulder" of the inlet is so narrow, the tide boils in with great force.

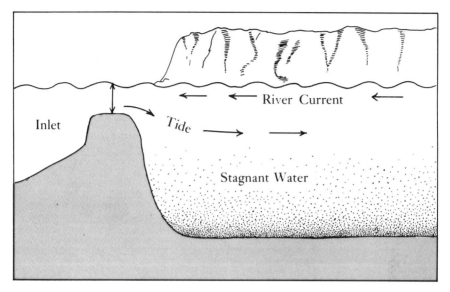

Circulation in a deep estuary.

In some places its speed has been logged at eight knots. The surface waters are churned up then, even at the "wrist" end. Within a few hours the water level inside the arm rises thirty feet or more.

When the tide turns, it seems as though someone had pulled the plug in a gigantic bathtub. Tumbling and foaming, the tide rushes out. And as it goes, it sweeps away branches and oil drums and other less visible debris. These substances too may end up as fine particles supporting life within the arm.

In a long shallow estuary such as Chincoteague Bay in Virginia, you hardly notice the changing tide. On a calm day water moves gently against the shore, leaving a rim of wet sand at low tide. Wind riffles the surface. Fish jump into the air. There is little other motion visible. All the same, the tide is catching and circulating nutrients from the land. Its gentle swells keep the trap working. For, deep or shallow, broad or narrow, sandy or rocky, an estuary is ruled largely by the surging tides.

However, the tide is not always the force that keeps a nutrient trap going. In some estuaries river currents may dominate the tides. The Mississippi River, for example, carries so much water that it freshens the sea in the Gulf of Mexico more than fifty miles from shore. Sailing outside the river mouth, the seventeenth-century explorer Esteban was able to take fresh drinking water from the sea. Here the mixing and trapping of nutrients occur mainly beyond the estuary in the sea itself.

At some seasons, almost everywhere, river currents become stronger and circulation patterns change. In northern estuaries this happens in the spring when melting ice and snow run off the land. Rivers rise and rush foaming toward the sea. Chesapeake Bay in Maryland, for example, catches water from many rivers. In the spring freshwater currents drive along under the tidal flow, surging seaward. Under this vigorous mixing, the salty layer may be greatly diluted within the estuary and for many miles outside it. At the same time the coldness of the river water affects its mixing within the estuary. The relatively warmer sea water tends to rise, and the cooler water to sink.

In summer, with its long hours of sunshine, the surface layers warm up. Water streams off into the air as vapor. With scant rainfall, rivers slow to a trickle. The water inside an estuary becomes saltier and saltier, sometimes saltier than the sea. This happens quite frequently in such southern estuaries as the Laguna Madre in Texas. In the warm briny waters the circulation of nutrients slows, sometimes with fatal results for the living inhabitants.

At any season, the workings of the nutrient trap may be affected by winds and waves. Wind blows the surface waters in waves against the land or drives them out to sea. This forces a flow of deeper water upward. And then, of course, nutrients from the bottom are recirculated.

The very forces that trap nutrients are continually altering the shape of the trap as well. For this reason it may be useful to see how the estuaries that now exist came to be.

3

Arms in the Making

On a cold day in midwinter, almost any northern estuary becomes a ghostly field. Tides rise and fall unseen beneath the pale green ice. Rivers hardly flow at all. Chunks of ice lean against shrubs, like crazy building blocks. Sea foam, frozen even as it flew, hides sand and rocks along the shore. The shape of the estuary is soft and blurred.

In the spring, as the ice melts, you find the shoreline altered. Rivers have carved away banks, ice has scoured out last year's sandbars, high tides have undercut great bulkheads. A slim sandspit is forming around a wrecked rowboat. The shaping goes on season after season, year after year. But because the process is so slow, the change is scarcely noticeable.

At least eight times in the past 400,000 years, the earth's climate has become extremely cold. The last such period ended about 17,000 years ago. Each time, the cold was followed by a warmer period like the one we are enjoying now. Many scientists believe that the present warm period is ending. If this is so, our coastline will again undergo some drastic remodeling.

Of all the mighty upheavals in the earth's history, probably the most dramatic changes in the coastlines were brought about because of ice. Winter after winter, blizzards roared over the northern part of our continent. Winds whirled snow into the air; cold mists hung over the sea. Even in summer the weather stayed cold, and the snow melted very little.

Year after year, snow fell on snow and became ice. The ice grew deeper and deeper. In places it was a mile thick. The land sank beneath its icy burden. From the mountains in the northwest, from Hudson Bay in the northeast, the ice began moving like rivers of ice.

These rivers of ice, or glaciers, advanced century after century, spreading southward into the heart of the continent. Scrunching across hills and plains, they tore away rocks and boulders, filled up valleys, scooped out lakes. Slicing down rocky cliffs to the seas, they carved out headlands and islands, inlets and sounds. In this way the jagged shorelines of the northeast and northwest were created.

The islands and estuaries of southern New England developed as the ice melted. If you have ever rolled a heavy snowball downhill, you have noticed that it picks up loose pebbles, dirt, twigs, and such things in its path. In much the same way, the glaciers gathered rocks and boulders and other debris in their long advance over the land. Along their southern edges where

27

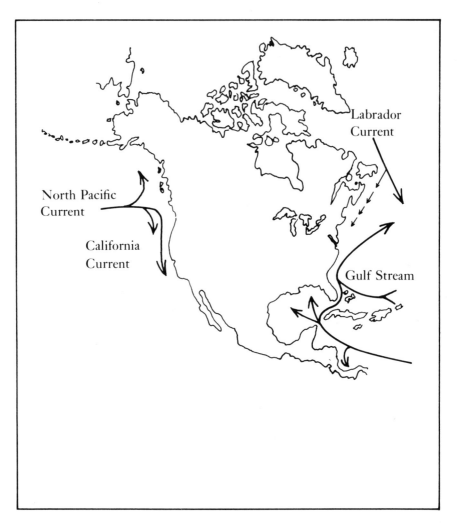

Pattern of ocean currents.

temperatures were warmer, the ice melted. Like giant snowballs, the melting sheets of ice left piles of debris.

Dropped in long ridges known as moraines, this debris forms the low hills of Long Island, Block Island, Martha's Vineyard, Nantucket, and other, smaller islands. A separate moraine runs along the north shore of Long Island to the elbow of Cape Cod. The lower parts of these ridges lie under the sea.

Across the moraines trickled pebbles, gravel, and sand. This lighter material formed the low-lying areas, or outwash plains, along the south shores of these islands. Melting water cut streams and rivers in the sandy plains. Many streams and rivers today still follow the old riverbeds.

The ice sheets melted along their southern edges and, slowly as the ice age ended, drew back. Farther and farther north the ice melted. It appears to be melting still. In this age-long "spring" thaw, the ice melted, melted, melted. And the melt water roared into rivers, poured into the sea. The sea level rose—and is still rising as the glaciers melt.

The sea rose very rapidly at first, pushing against the land. Wherever it found an easy opening, it fingered its way in. Its arms reached up the deep ice-carved basins like Puget Sound in Washington and Somes Sound in Maine. The sea rushed hundreds of miles up rivers, spilling over their banks. Drowned under the sea, ancient rivers and their valleys became estuaries. Chesapeake Bay on our eastern seaboard and Yaquina Bay in Oregon are two such drowned river valleys.

The rising sea covered former lowlands, creating an underwater shelf that slopes gently down to the deep ocean floor. In many places along the Atlantic and Gulf coasts, this continental shelf is 100 miles wide. Waves roll slowly along this shelf toward shore, and currents pulling along the shore tend to be weak. Offshore and longshore currents are also relatively weak

29

Ocean currents, moving along the shore, drop their burden of sand at the mouth of the Klamath River in California. The resulting sandspit is cut away in winter when heavy rains swell the river, and again the shape of the river mouth is changed.

along the northern and western coasts of Alaska. There the continental shelf is almost 400 miles wide in some places.

Along the Pacific coast, however, the shelf is mostly quite narrow. The coastal mountains, which themselves are still rising, present a steep wall of hard rock. There are few places where the sea can gain an opening into the land.

In general, land has been and still is being lost to the sea. Under some conditions, though, the rivers build up land, keeping back the sea. Along the east coast from Cape Cod to Florida, and along the Gulf coast, the land is low and sloping. Rainwater flows away as rain does off a roof in a series of almost parallel rivers, including the Susquehanna, the Potomac, the Roanoke, the Pee Dee, the Santee, and the Savannah.

Rivulets washing down a roof carry away dirt and other loose material. The rivers of the southeast wash rocks, sand, and other sediments off the land. Sometimes so many sediments collect downriver that a dam builds up across the river mouth. Many lakes and ponds along the south shore of Cape Cod and its neighboring islands formed in this way.

More often the loose material may be picked up and moved by the sea. As a wave breaks against the shore, it drags some material out to sea in its backwash. In places with a steady prevailing wind from one direction, narrow currents build up paralleling the shore. As they flow past, they move sand with them, molding it into long spits and bars. One such sandspit, called Monomoy Point, creeps steadily southward from the elbow of Cape Cod. Its shape shifts continually, depending on the force of winds and tides.

Similar spits and bars have developed more or less parallel to the shore all the way to the Rio Grande. Fire Island and Padre Island National Seashores, Chincoteague and Pea Island National Wildlife Refuges are among those located on and within such bars. Called barrier beaches, they protect the coastline from the full force of pounding surf and storm tides. In so doing, they enclose shallow bays and lagoons, whose calm waters nourish abundant seafood and wildlife. The

31

The Colorado River meanders southwestward through a wilderness of mountains, plateaus, and deserts before emptying into the Gulf of California. Here the river almost "chokes" on the sand and mud deposited during periods of high water flow.

Great South Bay in New York is perhaps the largest of these bays.

In the Gulf of Mexico, the rivers do more than provide raw material for sandspits and islands. They are building the mainland itself, filling in old estuaries and depositing the materials for new ones, which in turn become filled in. The wedge of land that builds up at the mouth of a river is called a delta, because it is shaped like the Greek letter Δ, or delta. On a map you can see bulges around the mouths of rivers, such as the Apalachicola, the Brazos, the Rio Grande, and of course the Mississippi. The Mississippi Delta alone grows at the rate of 300 feet a year. Its sediments may once have been part of the mountains—the Rockies in the west or the Appalachians in the east. Since the last ice age, soil from half the continent has filled in more than 100 miles of southern coastline. All of Louisiana and most of Mississippi were created by the rivers.

On the west coast, few rivers run off the continent into the sea. Those that do pour down through the hard rock of the coastal mountains and carry little sediment. South of Cape Mendocino, however, rivers have deposited much sand and silt, which longshore currents have molded into spits and bars. These protective bars enclose many small coves as well as larger estuaries like San Diego, Newport, and Mission bays. San Francisco Bay and the nearby Tomales Bay are unique, having been created by an earthquake fault.

The shaping of shore by earthquake and glacier, sea and river continues. Living beings too alter the shore. One thinks at once of people laying an earth dam across a stream or setting down a bulkhead or dike to separate land from sea. However, other animals also build up the shoreline. Most of Florida peninsula stands on an

Winds and waves shape Assateague Island—now digging out stumps of cedar trees killed and buried by storms, later perhaps hiding them again.

old coral reef. Certain small worms, settling on shells or other hard substances offshore, build tubes of sand around themselves. More worms attach themselves near the first settlers. As the colony, or group, becomes larger, their tubes form a massive reef, slowing down waves and thus protecting the shore.

As worms die, chunks of reefs may break off and be washed ashore. Sometimes you may find quite large pieces of the hard grayish sand lying on beaches like some weird rock from outer space. If you look at it through a magnifying glass, you can make out the small grains of sand and shell that were cemented together around each tube by the living worms.

In the earth's long history, however, plants have been more important than animals in shaping estuaries. Battered by winds, drenched by tides, flooded by rivers, carved by ice, the shoreline of an estuary would seem an uncertain place to make a home. Yet somehow, about 45,000 years ago, certain grasses did take hold in the damp mud and sand. Growing green and tall, they make a spongy edge between land and sea.

This beautiful fringe of green has made the dry land more habitable for land animals. And by hugely increasing the supply of nutrients available, the plants have made the estuary more habitable too. After a storm almost anyone can see—from the land side or the water side—how this is so.

1765476

4

The Marsh

In ancient times the people of India had a word for marshes, and their word has come down to us scarcely changed. Our word *marsh* comes from their ancient Sanscrit one *"mersc"*, which meant "full of seas." In any language the names for important things are not easily lost or changed. This suggests that so long as people have written their own histories, they have understood the importance of marshes. The wetlands, or marshes, formed a buffer zone that protected them from the raging sea and supplied them with food.

Everyone knows that the sea gives us food, such as fish, shrimp, and oysters. But how can a place full of seas protect us *from* the sea? This may take some explaining, for a marsh is certainly full of seas.

At high tide the sea glimmers among the marsh plants, reflecting cloud or moon. In stormy weather the tides rise even higher than usual. Driven by winds or swollen by rains flooding off the land, the sea may hide the plants altogether.

Almost always *Spartina alterniflora* is the first plant to take root in the mud or sand at the edge of the land. At high tide only the top of the grass shows above water.

At low tide, though, the marsh is uncovered. Its muddy brown soil looks bare, open to the sky. And this is especially so in early spring when ice has scoured away the stumps of last year's plants. Yet the soil is damp underfoot, and if you press your toes down firmly, water seeps over them. The sea is there. So the ground, barely above sea level, is always wet.

37

Along the shores of Glacier Bay, grasses are bathed in icy water. Here, as farther south, it is the tides that determine which kinds of grasses grow where.

Wet as it is, a few kinds of plants can grow here. They are not killed by salt, and their roots do not rot though they are always in water. Such plants "anchor" the low-lying marshes, and they are much the same whether in Alaska, Louisiana, southern California, or New York. For most marsh plants are grasses, though grasses of a very tough and special sort.

Along the coasts of Greece, such tough grasses were made into cords, called *spartinas*, used for fishing lines and nets. Scientists have given the name *Spartina alterniflora* to the grass that grows on sea-filled marshes of the east coast. It is also called cordgrass or saltmarsh grass as is the closely related kind that grows along west coast marshes. There are still other kinds of grasses in the *Spartina* group. Most grow on the higher marsh where they are soaked by the sea only during the unusually high or "spring" tides that "spring up" with the new and full moons.

Like lawn grasses, spartina seeds send roots down into the ground and stems up into the sunlight. Like other grasses, spartina sends stems out sideways under the ground. Each underground stem, which is called a rhizome, grows long and straight. At intervals it puts roots down and a stalk up, and runs on again as though trying to reach higher, drier ground. The new plants sprout new rhizomes, and they too run outward, away from the main stem.

Roots and rhizomes from one plant cross those from other plants. In this way a thick wiry mat is formed. Though the stems and leaves die back in winter, this underground mat lives on.

Canada geese and muskrats dig out spartina roots and eat them. But if you try to imitate these animals, you find the task more difficult than it looks. Besides, as food the roots are not very tasty.

39

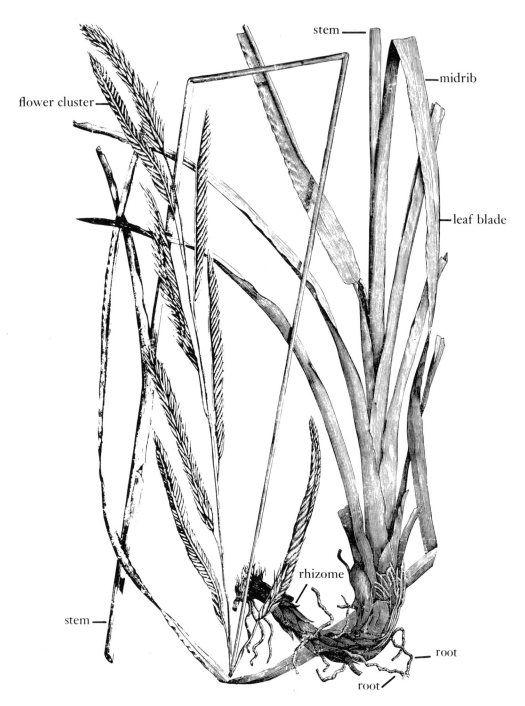

A typical spartina grass. Flower stem has been cut off so entire plant will fit on page. One leaf has been doubled over and bent around to suggest length of actual blade.

40

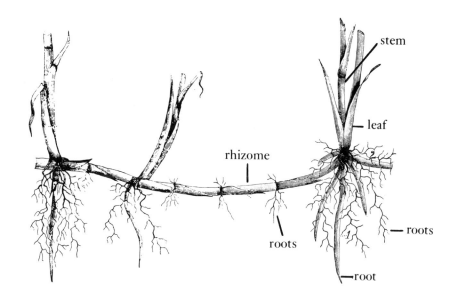

Detail of the underground parts of grass plant.

A Canada goose works its legs up and down, up and down, loosening the mud with its big webbed feet. Then its long black neck arches down, its bill shoves into the mud, and the bird plucks out a mess of starchy plant material.

You can loosen the soil around a clump of spartina without much trouble. But somehow no matter how hard you pull and tug, no matter how cleverly you work your fingers in among the roots, you come away with nothing but a handful of leaves. This does let you see how thoroughly the pale wiry roots and rhizomes are laced through the mud. And this lacing, of course, is what keeps the soil from washing away.

Even as the spartina grows, it collects more soil. During a rain, silt washes off the land. As it pours over the marsh, the grass slows its movement. Stopped

41

Anchoring the shores of Little Pine Key, Florida, red mangrove roots arch down into sand and mud and through the remains of an ancient coral reef.

by stems and leaves, the silt collects in tiny hills around the plants. Slowly the soil builds up, and so the level of the marsh rises. Unless there is a sudden rise in sea level or a long period of rain, the marsh holds the edge between estuary and land.

In tropical climates, like that of southern Florida, mangrove trees build up the shoreline. Mangroves are sometimes called "walking trees," because their roots seem to step out like stilts into the shallows. With the red mangrove (*Rhizophora mangle*) for example, roots sprout from the branches and from the trunk itself. They arch away from the tree, driving down into the mud. As the tree grows, its roots become new trunks, which in turn sprout roots.

In time there is a thick tangle of trunks and roots along the shore. This gives the slender tree support in strong winds and high tides. Like the spartina roots, this tangle catches and holds the soil.

The sea level is still rising and sediments are continually washing and blowing off the land. This means that the outlines and the level of any marsh are always changing too. To read the changing history of a particular marsh, botanists sink hollow tubes down into the mud. When they hit the underlying rock or gravel, they pull up the mud-filled tube as you might remove the core from an apple.

The marsh core is not a soft and gooey mass, but rather firm to touch. Stripes of dark mud and light sand alternate with the gray-brown remains of various plants, including seeds sometimes. Though pressed down by each succeeding layer of sand or mud, the dead plants do not disappear. For they decay only so long as they are exposed to air. As sediments sift over them, the process of decay slows and finally stops. As a result, the partly decayed plant material remains to add its chapter to the history of the marsh.

In the top layers, for example, a botanist may find only *Spartina alterniflora*, the cordgrass of the lower

43

marsh. Going deeper, he discovers a layer of eelgrass. Because this plant grows only when it is submerged in water, he knows that the present marsh lay below sea level at one time.

Going down still farther, the botanist identifies a layer of *Phragmites communis.* Though this grass can grow close to the water's edge, it cannot grow if its roots are regularly soaked by salt tides. Thus its presence shows that the estuary bottom was once above reach of the tides.

Underneath the layer of phragmites the botanist may sort out the remains of shrubs or trees, or perhaps of seaweeds and other material from the sea.

Pressed down, locked in by sediments, the dead plant material forms the substance known as peat. In older marshes, like those of Cape Cod, the peat may be many feet thick.

Walking over a marsh, you can almost feel the peat spring underfoot as though you were waltzing on a rather squooshy mattress. You sometimes sink in low places known as pannes or into ditches filled with rotting grass. But you do not sink in the marsh itself. The peat holds you up.

The marsh peat feels spongy. It also acts spongy. Strange as it may seem, it sops up fresh water and holds it. This is another way that the marsh keeps the dry land dry.

After a big storm, rainwater runs rapidly over the land, rivers spill over their banks, water rushes toward the sea. When it reaches the marsh, the flood seems

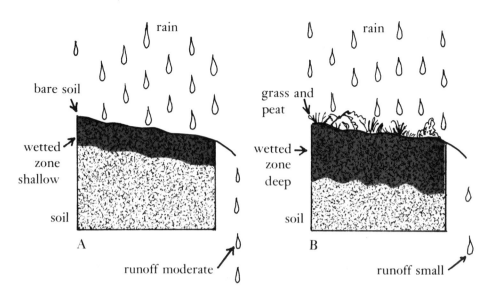

rain

bare soil

wetted
zone
shallow

soil

A

runoff moderate

rain

grass and
peat

wetted
zone
deep

soil

B

runoff small

Rain runs off bare land (A) and grass-covered land (B).

to disappear. A single acre of marsh can soak up 300,000 gallons of water, which is about as much as you could use in ten years. The marsh soaks up this water and releases it slowly into the estuary. The land is not torn away by the flood and, at the same time, the sea water is less rapidly diluted, thus letting sea creatures adjust more slowly to the change in salinity.

From time to time a rainstorm lasts so long that marsh peat and soil are thoroughly soaked. When they can hold no more water, then of course wetlands are flooded along with the dry lands above them. The floodwaters tear away the marsh edge, causing much damage. Fortunately, such severe storms do not occur every year. So most of the time the marsh can act as a sponge.

And because the marsh is full of water, it also acts as a watery sort of dike. It holds back the salt water, which the tide washes in twice each day. Thus it protects the fresh water in the ground above the marsh. In many coastal areas this is the water people use for drinking and washing and for watering their lawns.

To make your own profile of a salt marsh

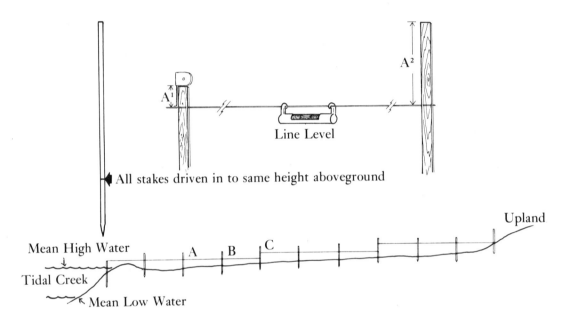

By choosing for study a small area of marsh bounded by a tidal creek and tall upland plants, you can follow the changes in plant life caused by differences in tidal range, groundwater salinity, and other environmental factors. One way to document your observations is to make a profile of the marsh itself.

You need little equipment: a line level such as carpenters use, measuring tape, 2 lengths of cord about 20 yards long, and a dozen stakes about 3 feet long. Bright red or orange paint makes your stakes more visible against the marsh.

46

If you have access to a school laboratory, you may want to test the water along the profile or transect. You will need a trowel, eyedropper, glass-marking pencil, and 12 plastic medicine bottles.

Either way, you will also need mosquito repellent. Some suntan lotions repel green-headed flies, which can be a nuisance.

The best time to work is at low tide when walking is relatively easy. Begin at the edge of the marsh and work upland. Drive the stakes into the ground at intervals of 10 or 15 meters or yards, depending on your tape. The height of the stakes aboveground should be the same in each case.

As you go, you will notice a change in the plant cover. Instead of the coarser *Spartina alterniflora*, the fine, silky-looking *Spartina patens* bends underfoot. You may also notice that the stake you are pushing down looks higher than the ones before it.

At this point take out the cord and line level. Tie the cord taut between the previous two stakes (A and B) and clip the level to it. Adjust the ends of the cord until the bubble in the level rests between the guidelines. Then measure the distance (A_1) between the cord and the top of each stake, and record it.

Now detach the cord from A and swing it around to go between stakes B and C. Make it level and measure the distance (A_2) between cord and stake top. This will give you a measure of the relative heights above the marsh floor, the mud flat, or whatever you take as a baseline. The difference in height between the stakes is a measure of how much the land has risen.

After you set out the last stake, dig a narrow hole next to it down to water. The level of the water below ground moves up and down with the tides. Draw up an eyedropper full of water and place a few drops on your tongue. This will give you a very rough idea of how salty the water is along the transect. In a school or other laboratory you may be able to determine the salinity by silver nitrate titration. To do this, take water samples from each hole, marking each bottle with the stake number. When the water is tested, you will have a profile of the water table paralleling the profile of the vegetation.

When botanists take up cores, water oozes into the holes. The cores are taken at intervals across the marsh from the lowest low-tide mark to the highest high-tide mark. Scientists then test samples of the water in each hole. From these samples, they can sketch a profile of the fresh water held in the sponge. The water has a wedge shape, flowing seaward along the wedge of salt water that pushes in. At the seaward point of the wedge, tiny amounts of fresh water trickle out into the estuary. This happens even as the tide goes out, even in hot, dry weather. This steady seepage helps keep the water from becoming too salty for organisms adjusted to life in the estuary.

Moving gradually upward toward dry land, the scientists find that the water becomes progressively less salty. In the last hole the water measures about 2 parts salt to one million parts water. Moreover, the water does not become any saltier even at high tide. At such low salinity levels, the water tastes sweet enough to drink. It does not harm the shrubby marsh elder and groundsel bushes that grow along the marsh. And in the higher ground just beyond, holly, pines, and sumac reach down to water sweet as rain. Salt spray prunes their branches, but so long as their roots can draw up fresh water, they thrive. These plants of the higher marsh also hold back the soil, keep the rain from washing it into the sea.

A sediment trap, a dam, an underground dike—the spongy marsh protects the land from the sea in all these ways. It keeps the dry land from becoming wet land. It keeps the water sweet. And it does still more.

Its plants use the nutrients, which are mixed with the sediments, and so can grow and build up the marsh. In so doing they provide food and shelter for goose and muskrat and many other animals. In turn they too become a source of nutrients for life in the sea. And so the life-giving cycle repeats its age-old pattern.

5

All Flesh Is Grass

"All flesh is grass, and all the goodliness thereof is as the flower of the field. . . . Surely the people is grass." So spoke the Old Testament prophet Isaiah.

Today as in biblical times, the grasses are the most important of all foods for people and for the animals that people eat. Corn, wheat, oats, rice, barley, sugarcane belong to the grass family. Spartina grass, too, is a very important source of food, though somehow the sight of its rice-pale, feathery seed heads bending in the wind does not convey "dinner" in quite the way the tassled heads of corn do.

True, the salt marsh looks like a field planted to some food crop. The ground is level and treeless; its boundaries are clearly set off by the curving shoreline and a sort of hedgerow marking higher ground. This hedgerow is formed by elder and other shrubs that grow on the drier ground of the upper marsh.

The spartina grows in clumps, each neatly spaced a hand's breadth or so from its neighbors, and connected

Spartina alterniflora

to them by the rhizomes. The blades are even in height, reaching to your ankles in June, to your knees in July, and higher still in August. Along drainage ditches and creeks, though, the grasses may grow a little taller. Even so, the marsh looks a smooth and level green.

In each green clump the leaves lean away from the stalk, spreading outward and upward like stiff fans. The stalk is hidden in the clasp of the leaves. The

51

leaf blades have sharp edges, tapering toward sharper tips. They sting your bare legs just a bit as you pass.

If you stop to look at a leaf more closely, you see that it bends inward slightly along its main rib. This gives it a slim boat shape. The outside is a deeper green than the inside. Both sides are well frosted with salt. If you touch your tongue to it gently, you can taste it. By giving off salts, which it cannot use, the plant stays in balance with its salty surroundings. And though a spartina blade is not very juicy compared to lawn grass, its juice, as you will discover if you chew one, tastes just as fresh.

Like the grass in a lawn, like the food grasses, like all green plants, the spartina leaves turn the sun's energy into food energy, or, to put it another way, they turn heat energy into chemical energy, something no animal can do. Their raw materials are air, water, and various minerals—all abundant in the open salt marsh.

In the sunlight the plant's green cells form carbohydrates, or simple sugars, by combining water from the soil and carbon dioxide from the air. In the process, which is called photosynthesis, oxygen is left over and released into the air and into the wet soil. This gas, of course, is the part of the air we need for life. With so many spartina plants giving off oxygen, the air in a marsh seems especially pure and sweet-smelling.

Each time the tides water the marsh, they deposit nutrients such as nitrates and phosphates. Drawing on these nutrients, the plants can also produce starches, oils, and proteins—chemical compounds that animals need and cannot make themselves.

The tides then fertilize and water the marsh simultaneously. They also drown insects that devour the spartinas. And since very few other plants can survive these daily soakings of salt water, you might say the tide "weeds" the marsh too.

In the light of the sun, the care of the tides, *Spartina alterniflora* produces food energy. It uses this energy for its own life processes, growing and producing seeds. However, it produces more energy than it uses during the growing season. The surplus is of course available to animals as food.

To measure this surplus, one scientist cut down the grass on an acre of marsh. When the stalks and blades were thoroughly dry, he had them weighed. The crop weighed about 20,000 pounds, or 10 tons. In terms of food energy, this is equivalent to 32,000,000 calories per acre. (You probably need about 2500 calories a day.)

This harvest was made at Sapelo Island, Georgia. Various marshes in Virginia seem to average about 5.1 tons. Marshes farther north, with their shorter growing season, probably produce somewhat less. So far no one has weighed a crop to find out.

These figures become more useful if we compare them to the yields from fields planted to crops. On the average, an acre of wheat may yield 1.5 tons of grain, an acre of corn 2.8 tons. Even rice and sugarcane plants, which are also grasses, do not yield as much food energy as the *Spartina alterniflora*.

And at that, the figures need some adjusting. On a farm, people must plow, plant, irrigate, fertilize, control weeds and insects, harvest, store, and finally sell the crop. In carrying out such activities, people burn up food energy and their machines burn up fuel, which is another form of energy. In a marsh, of course, the tides do all the work.

At no cost to anyone a salt marsh produces a great deal of food, which is used by animals including (though indirectly) people. All year long spartina becomes flesh.

A Canada goose, to mention just one example, may spend most of the winter on a North Carolina marsh; then it rests in many marshes along the coast in its migration north to breed before returning south again. It shelters among the spartinas, and it feeds on their starchy roots and rhizomes. It uses this food energy during its flight, in breeding, and in carrying on its other life activities. Some small amount of spartina energy is stored in its body, becomes part of its flesh.

In the fall a hunter may shoot the goose and eat it. He in turn receives some of the food energy produced by the spartina. The hunter is linked to the grass by the goose.

To illustrate this relationship, ecologists draw a simple food chain. The arrows indicate the direction in which the food energy flows, spartina⟶Canada goose⟶hunter.

Canada geese eat eelgrass and other kinds of plants as well as spartina. So they form links in other food chains as well. For that matter, spartina is eaten by other animals, from grasshoppers and mice to muskrats and deer. And of course the goose is not the only food eaten by the hunter.

A Canada goose defends her nest from the photographer whose boat comes too close. The roof of the muskrat lodge gives her a dry nesting site in the marsh.

If you tried to diagram all these interlocking food chains, you would end up with a tangled web of relationships. To give a less confused picture, diagrams are usually simplified with many organisms left out

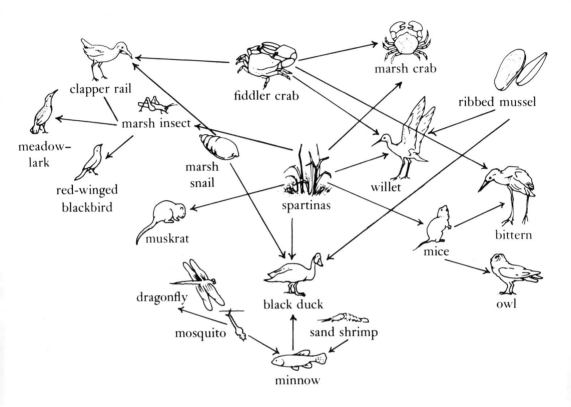

A simplified food web in a salt-marsh community.

but represented by others with similar feeding habits.

This food web of a salt-marsh community shows only a few of the plants and animals that live there. One organism, though, cannot be omitted: the vegetation, or spartina. Directly or indirectly, it nourishes each of the other organisms. In a tropical marsh, the mangrove tree occupies a similar place.

After the grasshopper and the goose and the deer have eaten their fill of spartina, much grass remains. The leaves and stalks turn yellow and fall to the ground.

Some are covered with sediments and in time become peat. About half of each crop, though, is carried away by the tides. Broken, waterlogged, decayed, it becomes the base for other food webs, webs that reach beyond the estuary to the open sea. And it becomes the main

Herons nest in mangrove thickets along the Everglades, feeding on crustaceans and small fishes, which in turn feed on decaying plant material from the mangrove trees.

source of nutrients that are circulated in the estuary trap.

To follow the tangled strands of this web whose beginnings are shown in the salt-marsh web, you need not go to sea. Exploring the edge of the marsh and the sloping mud flats that start where the grasses leave off, you begin to see the meaning of the biblical saying. In an arm of the sea, though, you might reword it. Here all seafood, fish and shellfish, is spartina.

6

The Spartina Story
Never Ends

In the early morning, spartina grass looms dim as a jungle as the tide ebbs away. If you row up a winding creek, you find the banks are exposed. Straight as a wall, they rise two feet or more from the muddy shallows up to the level of the marsh itself.

Here and there, currents have undercut the bank, leaving jagged shelves of peat. As if from some dark cave, blue crabs peer out, their big claws up, revealing pale undersides.

A dazzle of white bursts into the air as an egret lifts off, legs dangling, and disappears around a bend in the creek. The tall grasses shut out all view of the world beyond.

In some places the creek bank looks low enough to climb easily. But this is dangerous to try unless you know the marsh well. Instead of touching solid mud or sand, you may find yourself sinking into cold slimy muck. By the time you reach firm bottom, you may be waist-deep in dead and rotting grass.

Groping about with your feet for the sides of the hole, you feel mouths nibbling along your legs. Shrimp and other small crustaceans flick against your skin. You are stirring up their baby food. Perhaps, too, your legs have a special and appealing taste.

A pale jellyfish pulses slowly along. A silverside minnow shines within its belly sac. The hole teems with life, small and quick, animal eating animal. Their world is almost invisible, hidden in the murky water.

Then there is a sudden bubbling, a hissing sound like fat spitting in a frying pan. Dozens of fish, glinting blue-silver, almost black, rush across a narrow sandbar. They are mullet, blunt-nosed and large-eyed. Perhaps a ferocious young bluefish lurks beyond the bar. Or they may just be coming in for the baby food, fleeing no predator at all.

Here in the sheltering arm of the sea, with its huge and reliable supply of food, young mullet grow and develop along with many other animals. When they are fully grown, they go to sea to spawn, reversing the journey made by the salmon.

Mullet and almost all other animals sheltered in the estuary nursery depend on spartina in one way or another. However, the dead grass itself is too tough for even a large mullet with bony jaws or a young shrimp with its hard mouthparts. Before the grass can be eaten, it needs softening. The "cooks" who soften it up are the sea bacteria.

While some bacteria cause diseases, most kinds, including those that live in the sea, are anything but

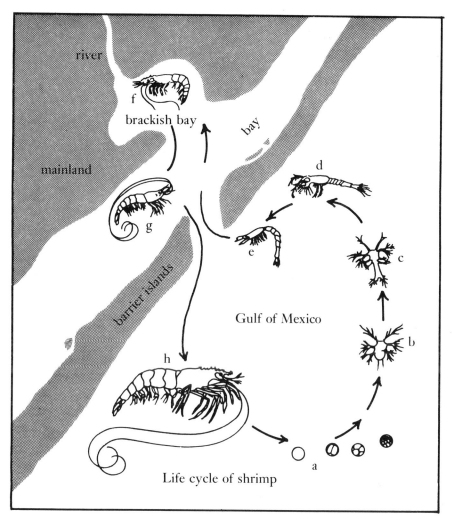

river

f

brackish bay

bay

mainland

d

g

e

c

barrier islands

Gulf of Mexico

b

h

a

Life cycle of shrimp

a, shrimp eggs; b-e, larval stages; f, juvenile shrimp; g, adolescent shrimp; h, adult shrimp.

harmful. For to get energy for their life activities, these bacteria feed on dead spartina and other dead organisms. In doing so, they break down the chemical compounds in these organic remains and make them available as food for young animals. In the end only inorganic minerals remain, and in this form become nutrients once more for growing plants.

Bacteria have extremely tiny bodies, consisting of

61

a single cell, with no mouths or stomachs. So the breaking down, or digesting, of the plant goes on outside their bodies. As their digestive juices soften the grass, the bacteria soak up food energy through their body walls.

The dead spartina nourishes the sea bacteria. At the same time the sea bacteria turn it into a more nourishing food. Instead of subtracting food value as they break it down, bacteria add it. This is because the bacteria coat the dead grass. As each tiny shrimp or mullet or worm feeds, it gets bacteria along with its meal. The coating of bacteria quadruples the protein value of the grass. The story is the same with dead mangrove leaves and other plant material that ends up in the sea. For this reason, sea bacteria are called living, or biological, multipliers. They increase the food value of the original material. And they do this not just once but several times, as you will see.

Tenderized and enriched by bacteria, the fine plant remains are called "detritus," which means "worn away." Spread around by the tides, the detritus sinks and lies on the bottom like a fine brown frosting. It collects in quiet creeks and in holes along the marsh edge. But seldom does it stay in one place for long. Wind and waves stir it about, as well as the tides. Each stroke of an oar or turn of a propeller or step of a foot mixes it around. The detritus is even circulated by animals that do not move about. One interesting example is the ribbed mussel (*Modiolus demissus*), a relative of clams and oysters.

Laced by spartina roots, the creek bank stands firm even at high tide. The abundant plant debris is filtered out of the water by the ribbed mussels, whose shells barely rise above the mud. (The one at the left has been removed from its bed for the camera.) Holes in foreground were made by soft-shelled clams which also filter out the detritus and, from time to time, expel unwanted particles.

If the bacteria are the cooks in this nursery, the ribbed mussels are surely the chief mixers and tasters. Clustered together among the spartina roots and in the peat along the creek banks, the mussels seem lifeless at low tide. They might be taken for odd lumps of mud or darkened stumps of dead grass. When the tide comes in, though, the mussels go to work. Their two shells open, revealing two small grayish tubes known as siphons. The mussel draws water in through one siphon and expels it through the other. It can pump about a gallon of water through its shells each hour. (To appreciate what a feat this is, see how long it takes you to drink the same amount—comfortably!)

This steady pumping creates a gentle current around the mussel shells. This current lifts detritus off the bottom, whirls it around, and draws it into the ingoing siphon. Once inside the mussel's body, the detritus-laden water passes over the mussel's gills, where the beating of small hairlike cilia keeps it moving along. The gills soak up oxygen from the water much like the gills of a fish. They also trap the detritus.

When the mussel is feeding, its gills become slimy with mucus. This mucus "strains" the detritus particles from the water as it flows over the gills. Then other cilia move the food-laden mucus toward the mouth. There particles too large or too tough to swallow are cast aside, and the rest is eaten.

Along some quiet creeks, the cast-out material almost buries the mussels. It may take a storm tide to flush the mussel bed clear. But meanwhile various other animals as well as bacteria remove the debris by making it part of themselves.

The discarded detritus still retains much food energy that living beings can use. So does the undigested portion that is excreted by the mussels. Each dead spartina blade probably is sorted over and passed through at least six animals before it is completely broken down. At each step, bacteria move in, feeding on the remains and increasing their food value.

With their front claws, fiddler crabs scoop up detritus and larger debris on the mud flats. The males must feed one-handed, though, for they use the large "fiddle" claw mainly to attract females to their burrows during the spawning season. The burrows, like the claw prints, let air into the marsh soil, so helping decay bacteria survive.

Here and there you may see small fiddler crabs scurrying over the mud flats, grabbing up spartina debris by the clawful. More likely they will hide from your heavy steps inside their burrows. Among the mussel beds and higher up on the marsh itself you may find the round entrances to their burrows. Sometimes you can touch a crab by sliding a finger gently under its "roof." Around the burrows you may also find scattered piles of discarded detritus. For the crabs, too, sort and sift through the detritus, crushing larger particles and throwing out any parts they cannot eat.

Drawn into the creek by an outgoing tide, these wastes settle on the bottom where an amazing number and variety of creatures trap them as food. These organisms range in size from microscopic bacteria and yeasts to mullet big enough for you to eat. (And when you do, the mullet of course becomes a link between you and the detritus!)

Some animals in the vast bottom community can be found very easily. Handsomely striped periwinkles cling to spartina blades, resting at low tide while their cousins, the mud snails, creep about, long siphons waving. Other kinds of animals, such as fat lugworms and burrowing sea cucumbers, can be found only by digging. It is not necessary to dig very deep, though, for the detritus they eat lies mixed with the top inch or two of bottom.

Other bottom-dwelling creatures are more elusive, being smaller and softer. But if you swim across the flats at high tide, you may glimpse some through a face mask. Long rubbery siphon tubes of tiny soft-shelled clams reach up to the surface. So do the plume-like gills and bright-colored feelers of various worms that also remain well down in the sand. Their hiding places are tubes that they build of mucus and sand or shells.

Animals like the mussels and these tube worms, which strain their food out of the water with gills, mucus, or similar structures, are known as "filter-feeders." The filter-feeding worms become food mainly for young shrimp and crab, fish, and birds. Many filter-feeding mollusks, such as oysters, clams, and the edible mussels, are also eaten by people. And again our link with the spartina detritus is very direct.

Elegant common or American egrets pace the mud flats watching for the gleam of crab or fish. Note their heavy spearlike bills.

With other kinds of seafood, such as shrimp and lobster, the links become more numerous and complicated. For shrimp and other crustaceans, the detritus serves only as baby food. As the young develop, they begin to feed on worms and on even smaller crustaceans. Most young fishes also start by eating detritus, then progress to more solid foods, including shrimp. But a young striped bass, for example, eats so many differ-

People, too, hunt the mud flats for food.

ent kinds of animals that enough of each survive to spawn and start the next generation on its way.

In this curious fashion the very number and variety of estuary animals protects each kind of animal. Though worm is eaten by shrimp and shrimp is eaten by fish, always some of each kind survive to reproduce. And the ample supply of spartina or mangrove leaves ensures that the story can continue.

Of course the spartina story does not stop with the animals. Though the food energy is used up by growing animals, minerals and other chemical compounds remain. Unlocked by bacteria from the once living leaf, they are circulated by the tides over the marsh and through the arm of the sea. Thus the mineral remains fertilize the young plants of the marsh and oі the sea—which in turn feed the young animals.

Whether in shallow southern lagoons or deep northern sounds, the story goes on and on in an endless cycle. This ceaseless exchange of materials and of energy between living organisms and their surroundings is known as an "ecosystem."

Nutrients flow without beginning or end from land to sea to land.

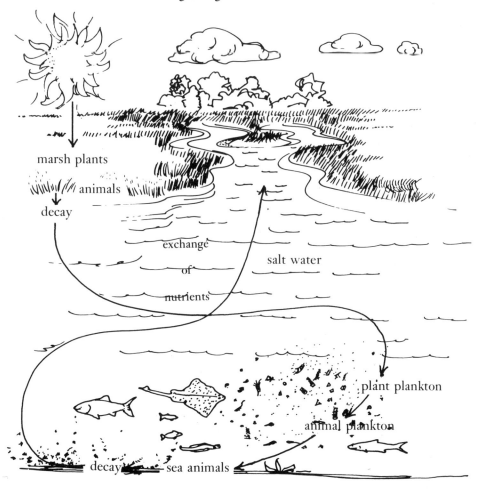

marsh plants

animals

decay

exchange
of
nutrients

salt water

plant plankton

animal plankton

decay — sea animals

7

The Invisible Plants
of the Estuary

When you walk in a forest, it is easy to step on soft mosses and low weedy herbs without really noticing them. Unless the undergrowth is unusually thick or thorny, you are much more aware of the tall trees above your head.

In a marsh, it is also easy to miss the undergrowth. This is so even if you are looking for it, because usually it is visible only as a pale green or golden brown. This color comes from plants so tiny that you cannot see them without a microscope. They are mud algae, which have no stems or leaves or flowers. Their bodies consist of a single cell.

Invisible except in large clusters, the mud algae grow wherever they can get the light, air, water and nutrients needed for growth. They grow on the damp ground beneath the spartina plants and along the bare creek banks, on the shells of the ribbed mussels, and on the grass blades themselves. They grow singly or in soft jellylike sheets of shapeless clumps of dark green. Sometimes these sheets have a rather oily shimmer.

Unlike the marsh grasses, mud algae can grow all

70

Marine scientists use fine-mesh nets shaped like bongo drums to sample fish larvae and other plankton at various depths. Samples are studied in laboratories, both on the research vessel and onshore.

year long. During the winter, when the grasses die back, the marsh mud is open to the sun. So though the hours of sunlight are fewer, the mud algae may actually get more light. And at low tide, when the sun warms the soil, they can make food and grow.

In more northerly estuaries where marshes freeze over, the algae remain in a resting state, ready to "sprout" when warm weather comes. In the tropics, where growing conditions are much the same all year, the algae keep growing, millions upon millions of them. Crowded together beneath the mangrove trees, they look like a thick yellow-green carpet. In this thick mass, each individual plant is invisible.

Though dwarfed by mangroves or grasses, the tiny mud algae produce a surprising quantity of food energy. For every three tons of spartina, a marsh may yield one ton of mud algae. A soft, nourishing food, this crop is eaten by marsh and water animals, and when broken down and decayed, it supplies nutrients for plants growing in the estuary waters. Then these plants, too, become food for animals.

Of the estuary plants, both large and small, it is the tiny one-celled algae that produce the most food. In vast areas of the sea they are the only food producers, making up in numbers for the smallness of their size. Because arms of the sea function as nutrient traps, they can support even more one-celled plants than can the open sea. For of course the very forces that trap the nutrients trap the tiny plants as well.

Lacking roots or other means of clinging to the bottom, the microscopic plants drift about with winds and currents and tides. They form a sort of floating pasture in which uncounted small animals graze. As a whole, this floating sea life is known as "plankton," from a Greek word that means "wandering." However, the tiny plants do have some control over where they are going.

72

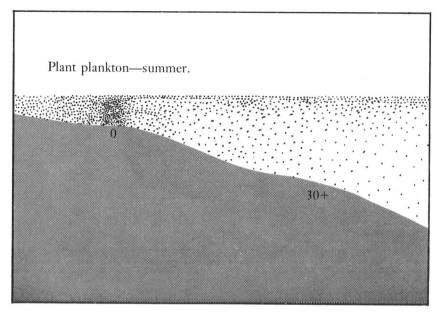

Plant plankton—summer.

0

30+

In summer microscopic plants drift near the surface in areas where salinity is low. Salinity from 0 to more than 30 parts per thousand.

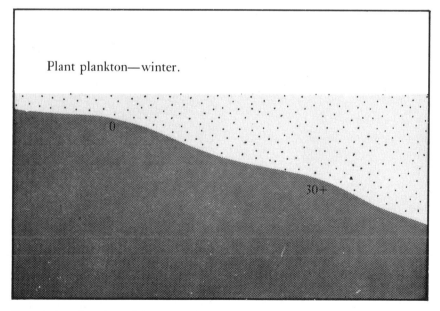

Plant plankton—winter.

0

30+

In winter the tiny plants are fewer in number and more evenly spread through the water.

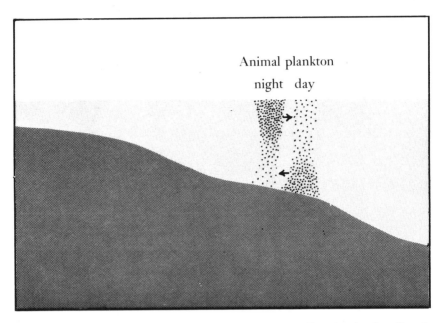

Microscopic animals, including larvae of almost all animals that live in estuaries, drift inland during the day and seaward at night, tracing a roughly circular path through the water.

By sampling the water at different times and in different parts of an estuary, scientists have discovered that the plant plankton tend to remain in water of a salinity and temperature that best supports their growth. During the day the plants drift to warmer, less salty waters at the inland end of the estuary. At night they are found in greater numbers at the seaward end, where the water cools off more slowly. By sinking somewhat, the plants avoid being swept out to sea.

As daylight approaches, the plant plankton rise toward the surface. In shallow waters they are found all the way to the bottom, since even there they can get enough light for growth. Scientists believe that the tiny plants can adjust to their surroundings in other ways, too, but these are not yet well understood.

To collect samples of plankton, scientists use nets with very fine mesh. They tow them behind boats at various levels from the bottom of an estuary to the surface. The most abundant of the plants they find

Moving its broad flat bill back and forth through the water, a roseate spoonbill sifts out the tiny crustaceans that are its food. These creatures in turn feed on tinier animals which feed on microscopic mud algae, visible as a thick mat of green along the high-tide line.

Fish larvae (A) and eggs (C), (E), copepods (B), and crustacean larvae (D), (F) — here greatly magnified — are among the billions of young creatures making up the animal plankton.

are the diatoms, a name meaning "cut in two." Each diatom has a glassy two-part shell, which is often compared to a pillbox with a close-fitting lid.

These "pillboxes" come in many shapes, each suited to floating in water. Some diatoms grow in colonies, forming long chains like bracelets. Most occur singly like invisible jewels in the sea. Sometimes these jewels become so numerous that the sea looks green or, strangely, yellow or brown. It may even glow a deep pink as if bathed in a day-long sunset. The water feels "thick," almost heavy, when you pass your hand through it.

At such colorful moments the plankton is said to be "blooming." The blooms usually occur along the coast in late winter and early spring when supplies of nutrients are at their greatest. Currents rising from the bottom sweep nutrients up into the light-filled layers of water. And of course melting ice and rains wash them off the land. Even along a marshy shore where the supply of nutrients is fairly steady all year long, there is a tremendous increase in nutrients in the spring.

At the same time, days are longer. Plants have more hours of sunlight in which to grow. Diatoms then may double in number every twenty-four hours. During such blooms, scientists estimate, there may be more than 70,000,000 diatoms in a cubic foot of water.

The spawning of many sea animals is timed to the seasonal blooms of diatoms and other plant plankton. When the young hatch, food is all about them. The hatchlings are not much larger than the diatoms, but as with the tiny plants, their enormous populations make up for their small size.

The animal plankton are not only small and numerous, but also extremely varied in kind and life habits. This is especially true inside estuaries because so many animals spawn there. As for animals that spawn outside, ocean currents carry their young into the estuaries, and so those creatures too are trapped there.

In plankton samples taken one spring day from the

77

Great Peconic Bay in New York, scientists found the eggs of many fishes as well as newly hatched fish. With a microscope they identified the immature forms, or larvae, of porgyfish (scup), mackerel, weakfish (sea trout), blowfish (puffer), flounder, herring, anchovy, and menhaden (mossbunker) to name just a few. Along with the fishes the scientists netted the larvae of sand shrimp, blue, spider, and oyster crabs, barnacles, and many other crustaceans including copepods and ostracods. In addition they collected mollusk larvae, sponges, sea squirts, worms, and jellyfishes. Most of these creatures were microscopic in size, except for some jellyfishes as big as plates. In all, the scientists identified about 3000 different kinds of organisms in a one-quart sample.

These plankton animals feed on the diatoms and other microscopic plants. They also feed on smaller animals —and are eaten by larger ones. Unless you tow a plankton net through the water, you get little sense of all this teeming life, however. On a clear summer day in a shallow lagoon the water may seem empty of life. This is because most plankton animals are as clear as water and many never grow big enough to be seen without a microscope. Those that do grow bigger leave the plankton by the time they can be seen. After developing to a certain size, they are ready to live as their parents did. Fishes swim away, for example, while other animals such as clams and sea urchins settle to the bottom.

Wading in the warm estuary water, you may feel worm tubes underfoot, crisp and brittle in contrast

Like their larger relatives, shad, herring, and sardines, tiny anchovies feed on plankton. They swim along with their mouths open, and as water runs over their gills, gill rakers strain out the food. For greater safety anchovies move in schools, crowding still closer together if attacked.

to the soft bottom ooze. These worms still depend on the plankton as food. Schools of small fishes race along, then turn suddenly as if but one fish, and dart off in another direction. The fishes may be herring or menhaden, they too dependent on plankton all their lives.

This plankton food remains invisible to the human eye, yet one fish may eat 50,000 copepods as you are watching the movements of the school. And each cope-

After a successful dive a royal tern returns to its colony on an island in Matagorda Bay, Texas. It takes many pounds of fish to feed even a small colony of terns, perhaps ten times their weight in crustaceans to nourish the fish, and ten times more plants to feed the crustaceans. The original food producers greatly outweigh and outnumber the consumers at the peak of this food pyramid.

80

pod, though smaller than a spartina seed, may eat 120,000 diatoms in a day. The diatoms are smaller than the copepods, of course, and the copepods are smaller than the fish that eats them. Because they are so small, it takes a great many diatoms to feed each crustacean and a great many crustaceans to make each fish feel full. Besides, each consumer, whether copepod or menhaden, uses up most of the food energy in growing, moving about, spawning, and so on. So perhaps only one tenth of the energy a copepod gets from the diatoms is available to the menhaden, and less than one tenth of that will be available to the bluefish that devours the menhaden.

While food chains and webs show who eats whom, they do not show how much gets eaten at each step of the way. To illustrate better such food-energy relationships, scientists use "food pyramids."

In an estuary, the diatoms and other microscopic plants form the base of one food pyramid. They number in the billions and weigh in the tons. At the next level are millions of one-celled protozoans which eat the plants. These are consumed by thousands of microscopic and larval crustaceans, which in turn are eaten by hundreds of fish fry and small fishes. At the next level of the pyramid are the tens of larger fishes that feed on the smaller fishes, and, at the peak, a human consumer perhaps.

Moving up the food pyramid, the organisms tend to become fewer and larger. The largest animal ever to live on our planet feeds entirely on some of the

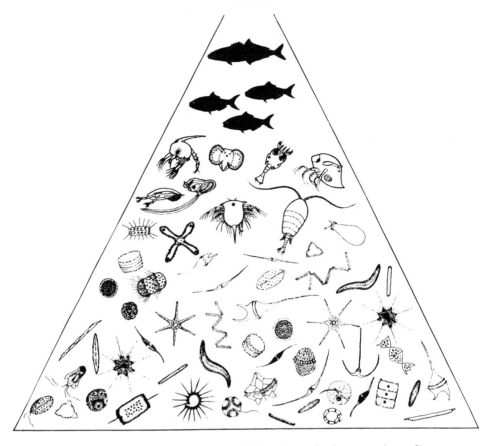

A food pyramid. Its base is supported by plant plankton, such as diatoms and dinoflagellates. Larvae, tiny copepods, and even tinier plankton animals feed directly on the plants. They are eaten by menhaden, which in turn are preyed upon by bluefish. Above the bluefish is space for the final consumer—you.

smallest. The great blue whale eats tiny crustaceans that feed on the tinier copepods. The whale shark, which is the largest living fish, also feeds on small plankton animals as do its relatives the basking shark and the manta ray. Because these food chains are so short, relatively little energy is lost from microscopic plant to ultimate consumer. Even so, a whale weighing 100 tons must consume unimaginable amounts of plankton. So far as I know, no one has calculated how many tons of plankton are needed to support a single whale.

82

Of course there are few of these gigantic animals and none in shallow estuaries. Most plankton eaters may be weighed in grams or, at most, a few pounds. Still, the total weight of the plant plankton greatly exceeds the total weight of all the plankton eaters, gigantic and tiny. This makes a solid base for the food pyramid.

Estuaries support tremendous populations of fish and shellfish because they trap and sustain enormous quantities of plant food. With the invisible algae of plankton and marsh mud added to the abundant detritus, estuaries are far more productive than the open sea. Of course some are far more productive than others. On the average, though, they are estimated to be twenty times more productive than the sea itself.

Except in very localized areas, the larger seaweeds and water grasses contribute relatively little to their total productivity. These plants are too tough for most animals to eat, and when they die they are usually washed ashore or covered with sediment before they can become detritus. They have a different but important role in estuary life.

8

The Visible Plants

During storms, great brown seaweeds may be torn loose and washed ashore. Walking along the beach, you find tough, ropelike fronds of *Chorda* and smooth, rubbery kelps many feet long. You may gather branching rockweeds, or *Fucus*, by the armful. Their beadlike air sacs are fun to pop as the plants dry.

These and other large algae are common in rocky estuaries. Indeed it is hard to imagine such places without them. Anchored to rocks and shells, to other seaweeds, to dock pilings and mooring lines, they bend and sway with currents and tides. Seeming one with sea and rocks, they create a special world for other sea organisms.

Vast beds of kelp form forests in cold waters. Among the huge fronds, small fishes and other animals can escape from swifter, fiercer predators. Closer inshore, featherweeds and rockweeds protect small sea animals in much the same way. Rockweeds especially are familiar, hanging at low tide like limp curtains over the

84

At low tide, conelike barnacles close their two-part "doors." Other animals are protected by rockweeds and (lower down) by bladder wrack. Knotted wrack lies in tangles across rocks in the background. Can you tell which rocks are most battered by surf?

rocks. Because the living seaweeds are slippery, you must watch your step if you explore the world beneath their sheltering fronds. The small creatures living there cannot swim away or burrow out of sight, so the wet slipperiness protects them from land animals like you. And it protects them from dry air and hot sun.

Parting the fronds, you can see various small animals clinging to rock and weed. Their activities for the most part stop until the tide comes in again. Only the periwinkles go on moving. They crawl over the damp rock and seaweeds, feeding on the microscopic algae attached to them. Amphipods jump like jittery shrimp away from the sunlight. Small crabs hold to seaweeds with prickly claws, their drab green-brown making them hard to see. Limpets press their fleshy feet against the rocks. The suction holds their conical hat-shaped shells so tightly that your fingers cannot work them loose.

You may also discover blue mussels held in place by threads spun from glands in their soft bodies. Sea anemones whose tentacles reach out at high tide like flower petals now look like pale lumps of hard jelly glued to the rock. Almost surely you will see barnacles and worms with hard white tubes. Once part of the plankton, these animals settle down on the rocks and cement themselves fast. They have no need to crawl about, since the incoming tide brings them the tiny plankton organisms they eat.

Such creatures and many more stir to life when the tide covers seaweeds and rocks again. But then the battering waves make their world difficult to observe.

For animals that live among the sea grasses, however, the movements of the tide make far less difference. The sea grasses they feed on grow mainly in sandy estuaries. They are not algae, but "pondweeds" which have become adapted to living in and entirely under salt water.

With their long narrow leaf blades and wiry roots, they look much like spartina grasses. And like them, they produce flowers that bear seeds, which sprout into new grass plants. Mostly, though, the sea grasses spread, like spartina, by means of their rhizomes across the soft sandy or muddy bottom. They may grow in depths of thirty feet or more, so long as the water is clear enough for sunlight to reach their leaves.

There are several kinds of sea grasses, including turtle, shoal, and manatee grasses, which are common along the Gulf and northern Atlantic coasts, and eelgrass (*Zostera marina*), which is common almost everywhere else. Shoalgrass, as its name implies, grows in very shallow water and may be uncovered at low tide. Manatee grass was named for the sea cows that graze on it—in great numbers once. It differs from the other sea grasses in having cylindrical blades rather than flat ones. Turtle grass is enjoyed by green sea turtles, while widgeon grass, which needs fresher water, is named for the water bird that feeds on it.

Inshore or off, the underwater meadows shelter many kinds of sea animals. Some, such as tiny hydrozoans and mosslike bryzoans, fasten themselves to the leaf blades. Their tiny tentacles give the grass a fuzzy look.

Still other animals crawl across the bottom, burrow down among the roots, or swim slowly through the grasses. You can visit this world with a face mask and snorkel.

Scallops, quickly jerking their shells open and shut, jet past, while a small black eel snakes its way over the bottom. A spider crab scrambles away from your shadow. When it stops moving, it "disappears." It can do this because it keeps its spiny shell covered with seaweeds, sticking on new pieces as the old ones break off or die.

There are many snails creeping slowly over the bottom and much smaller ones hanging on the grass blades.

Minnows and blue-eyed scallop feed among the eelgrass. The scallop's eyes appear as black dots in this underwater photograph. The fringes are sensitive organs of touch.

They are so tiny that their weight does not bend the grass. Perhaps, if you are lucky, you will discover a pipefish resting head-down among the grasses. Its body is so dark and thin that you may mistake it for a blade of grass. Like its cousin the sea horse, it feeds on plankton that drifts in and is caught among the grasses.

Lacking the pipefish's camouflage, most other fishes swim quickly away from you. Still, the tangle of sea grass protects them from most enemies. Larger fishes cannot move easily in pursuit.

Down among the roots, you may find quite a different world of animals. Wriggling your fingers in the sand, you lift out a stiff sand cone made by a trumpet worm or the long straight tubes of bamboo worms. Ribbon worms, slimy as overcooked noodles, and bloodworms too burrow there. And all about are the holes of various clams, soft-shells and hard-shells and tiny tellins with their long thin siphons.

Your list of discoveries can go on and on. The larger the grass bed, the longer your list is likely to be. Often clam diggers and fishermen can show you or tell you of other animals they find in the deeper waters where they work.

But even while digging clams or netting crabs in eelgrass beds, people may complain about the grass itself. It gets tangled around propellers or sucked into intake pipes of outboard motors. And as its growing season ends, dead grass drifts ashore and accumulates in slowly decaying piles. Then almost everyone wishes the bothersome grass would vanish forever.

89

In 1931 this wish seemed granted—along the Atlantic coast at least. A slimy fungus disease attacked the eelgrass. Almost all the grass died.

Five years later a scientist who had been studying eelgrass communities visited a former undersea meadow. He found mud snails and periwinkles creeping about as before. But the more active animals such as scallops, shrimp, and crab had disappeared. There was no grass now in which to hide. And of course the animals and plants that live attached to grass were gone.

Things had changed down in the bottom as well. Without roots to hold it, the sand and mud had shifted, burying the former clam beds. Digging into the soft bottom, the scientist did find some worms and clams, but not nearly so many individuals as before. Nor were there as many different kinds. Like so many other things, the eelgrass was not truly appreciated until it was gone.

The loss very nearly meant the extinction of the American brant, a waterfowl that eats almost nothing but eelgrass leaves and stems. So as the eelgrass vanished, the American brant went hungry. Weakened by hunger, these birds had little resistance to disease and little strength to escape foxes and other predators. Few could make the long spring flights north to the estuaries of the Arctic where the eelgrass was healthy. The related black brant thrived as before, since the disease did not reach its feeding grounds on the Pacific coast.

Even on the east coast, waterfowl that eat a variety

At low water the American brant tears up its favorite food and then, as the tide rises, drifts along eating it.

of foods did not suffer so greatly as the brant. Black ducks, for example, do eat much eelgrass. They also eat insects and snails as well as other plants. With the loss of the eelgrass, one strand in their food web was broken. Other strands remained. Thus though the food web was weakened, it did not collapse.

As it happened, the eelgrass began to recover and with it the brant and estuary organisms as well. Even before this, some brant had found a new source of food in a green seaweed that grows in shallow arms of the sea. Perhaps you have seen long stringy *Enteromorpha* and *Cladophora* or the wide lettucey *Ulva*, which may grow attached to the shells of living or dead animals, to old bottles and cans, to rocks and other sea-

91

weeds. In any case, the brant found them and fed on them during the eelgrass blight.

Today eelgrass and other sea grasses are disappearing again on all coasts, and with them the creatures they shelter and feed. This time the cause is not disease but people.

People have always been attracted to the arms of the sea where food is plentiful and easy to catch, where boats can safely anchor, where water is good for swimming. But as more and more people use estuaries for more and more kinds of things, their activities cause stress within the living world. By dredging a boat channel, they destroy eelgrass. Then there is not enough food for the brant that eat the eelgrass, the fox that feed on the brant, and so on. Thus, a small change can weaken food webs that stretch through an estuary from land to sea to land.

The following chapters will examine some of these changes and the stresses that result. People cannot stop all activities that injure estuary life. But they should become aware of the injuries and limit activities that threaten to destroy the entire ecosystem.

9

Digging up the Bottom

Clink, bink, clunk! With an uneven rhythm, shells tumble against the metal pipe. Sand hisses through and falls in a steady stream. The engine throbs and wheezes as it pumps up the estuary bottom. Such sounds mean a boat channel or perhaps an oil well for people, but only trouble for sea life.

From close inshore and from floating platforms farther out, powerful dredges shovel or draw out the bottom like enormous vacuum cleaners. By deepening the bottom, the dredges alter the shape of the estuary, the nature of the bottom, and the quality of the water. And as you may suppose, such physical changes inevitably affect the creatures that live there. This is true both while the digging goes on and long after the machines are stilled.

At one time or another, and for many reasons, dredging has been done in most large arms of the sea and in many small ones. It is done to get sand and gravel needed for construction of roads and houses. People

Hydraulic, or suction, dredge deepens a channel. The parallel "arms" along the pipe provide support and buoyancy. Sometimes a vinyl curtain, held by floats at the top and weights along the lower edge, is used to keep sediments from reaching productive estuary bottoms.

also mine estuaries for other raw materials such as oil, phosphate rock, sulfur—and even gold. More commonly, they dig to clear a way for boats and ships. Freighters, tankers, warships, and some commercial fishing vessels need depths of 45, 50, or even 60 feet to stay afloat. The harbors where such ships unload must be wide as well as deep, so that ships can anchor while they wait to unload. The port of Houston, Texas, and its shipping channel were created entirely by dredging. They would not exist without it.

For the new supertankers, such naturally deep harbors as the port of New York may not be deep enough. To allow such giant ships to navigate, channels will have to be blasted, not dug, through the underlying

94

rock. And no one quite knows what the effects of such "dredging" would be.

Of course channels do not need to be deep for small pleasure boats. However, a single arm of the sea may have a great many small channels, cutting across shoal areas. These small channels may alter an estuary's shape as much as a single deep one would.

Any channel, large or small, starts filling up as soon as it is dredged. Sand, mud, dead plant material slide in along with wrecked boats, broken fishing gear, and all sorts of rubbish. Before long the channel needs to be dug out again. And the more important a channel is for shipping, the more often this must be done.

The digging itself and the resulting change in shape disturb the rhythms of estuary life. This is obvious enough for the organisms in the path of the shovel or blades. As a dredge works across an estuary, it up-roots sea grasses and breaks off seaweeds. It dislodges clinging and bottom-dwelling animals and destroys others that move too slowly to get away. Gulls and other sea birds gobble up the victims, so—at least while it is going on—the dredging benefits them.

The dredge also affects organisms that live beyond its jaws. As you know if you have ever dug a hole under water, digging stirs up mud and sand. The longer you go on digging, the cloudier the water becomes and the longer the sand and mud particles take to settle. In its effects a dredge—particularly the shovel type—is like thousands of people digging. And so long as the monster digs, the sediments have little chance to settle.

Because these sediments cloud the water, they cut down the amount of sunlight reaching plants, the large seaweeds and grasses and the microscopic algae alike. As a result, the plants grow more slowly, and this of course reduces the food supply for animals.

Carried seaward, the sediments slowly settle out, causing more trouble. The heavier particles settle first, while lighter ones drift farther from the dredging site. Just how far they go depends on the strength of river currents and force of the tides. Thus silt tends to build up more in some areas than in others.

Filter-feeding animals are perhaps first to suffer under the stifling load. As a clam, say, pumps water in and out, fine silt as well as food sticks to its gills. And when the gills become coated with silt, the clam can neither breathe nor feed. The silt may bury fish eggs, so smothering the developing fish. Even a quarter-inch of silt makes the bottom too soft for most bottom-dwelling animals to move through. Their tunnels fill up as fast as they can make them. Cut off from oxygen and food, they too die. And the animals that depend on them for food may also die unless they can find something else to eat. The damage goes on and on as the layers of sediment deepen. In some places the bottom may become a deep and lifeless muck.

Life-smothering sediments come from land and not just from dredging. Wastes and nutrients mixed with these sediments affect estuary life also. For this chapter it is simpler to consider only the particles of sand and mud and clay.

Dragline breaks up bottom material and lifts it out of the water. Bulldozer helps prepare the shore for a concrete embankment.

With better channels and harbors, people need better docks to unload fish and other goods. They need factories and refineries to process them, new warehouses to store them, more roads and airports to carry them away. Before such things can be built, land must be cleared. So even as the dredges gobble up productive mud flats and marshes, bulldozers gobble up the land. This of course allows the soil to wash more swiftly away. Each year about 1,000,000 tons of silt flow into the Potomac River as a result of construction around Washington, D.C., alone. A big storm may wash in that much in a single day.

Along canals in Boca Ciega Bay, Florida, sediments from dredging and from building on land have piled up in layers four feet thick. To assess the effects of such activities on bottom life, scientists took bottom samples from these canals and from the natural undisturbed areas in the same bay. Collecting only the mollusks, both snails and clams, they identified 156 different kinds in the natural areas, but only five kinds in the canals. There were about 60 living animals in each natural sample as compared with an average of *one* live animal in the dredged samples. In some of the dredged material they found only the shells of dead mollusks.

The smothering burden of sediment is surely the most damaging result of dredging. But it is not the only one. Dredging affects plant and animal life in other ways too.

For one thing, the channel or hole, or even the pipeline from an offshore well, is a physical barrier. In this it is not so different really from the deep trenches made at some zoos to separate bears or lions from people—except that in an arm of the sea, predator and prey may find themselves on the same side of the trench. Its escape cut off, a young mackerel, for example, may have no chance of fleeing the wading bird that probes in the shallows.

Temperature too, as much as depth, may prove a barrier. Being deeper, the channel tends to be cooler. The coldness does not harm the animals so much as it changes their behavior. For many animals it may prevent spawning. It may keep young animals from moving to their normal feeding waters.

Then, too, the channel may let in predatory animals along with the boats. Large fish with big appetites can swim freely where once they were stopped by a tangle of grasses.

Worse still, the channel speeds up the flow of salt water into the estuary. It flows faster and in greater volume than before. Even as more salt water is coming in, there is nearly always less fresh water to dilute it. The factories, homes, and farms that grow up nearby need fresh water. To get it, people dam rivers or pump out ground water that normally seeps into the sea. The flow of fresh water may be slowed or cut off altogether. Sometimes the culprit is simply a badly planned highway like the one across the marshes of Louisiana and Mississippi.

A dam or a highway cuts off the flow of fresh water. It may also cut off the flow of sediments that build up the shore. And this, strangely enough, may mean more dredging. For now sand from farther out must be dug up and brought inshore to replace sand that the rising sea carves away from beaches.

Sometimes great barriers are built outside harbors as protection against storm waves, and these may cut off the flow of salt water. As a rule, though, most such structures have the reverse effect.

With more salt water and less fresh water, the salinity within the estuary changes. The water tends to circulate

Short tube "feet" on the underside of the starfish's arms can grip both shells of a scallop, clam, or—as here—an oyster. By pulling steadily, the starfish can wear out the mollusk. When at last it gapes open, the starfish feeds.

in new patterns, which in turn changes the movement of nutrients. It may mean that some shallow areas are buried in plant remains and other wastes while some are flushed so clear that they can support little life.

As salinity increases, it causes other problems too. Some animals like blue-claw crabs can tolerate a wide range of salinity. Others are much more limited. Jellyfishes and starfishes need water that is almost as salty

100

as the sea. A permanent rise in salinity offers such predators a new home—at the expense of animals already living there.

Walking along the beach, you may have seen empty clam shells pierced, each one, by a neat round hole. The hole is made by the small oyster-drill snail. Its long file-like snout can rasp through the hard shell and scrape out the flesh inside. While this snail can survive in salinities as low as 12 parts per thousand, it thrives, as do its victims, at salinities of 20 or 25 parts per thousand. Thus clams and oysters have a better chance of growing up when lower salinity keeps down the drill population.

Here a park naturalist at Acadia National Park in Maine shows two visitors a starfish and another of its favorite foods, the edible blue mussel.

Young fishes, shrimp, and crab must have low salinities in their early stages. A striped bass, for example, develops best in water that is nearly fresh. So as an arm of the sea becomes too salty, such animals must go farther upriver. There they may find the right sort of water, but not enough detritus to grow on.

In time the populations of shrimp and bass begin to decline, and with them the birds and mammals that depend on them. Again a single event—the change in salinity—triggers a whole chain of events, which seldom favors living creatures.

The problems caused by dredging cannot really be separated from the problems caused by getting rid of the material dredged up. When people mine the bottom for sand or oil, they of course want what is taken out. With channels, though, the dredged material is simply spoil—waste material no one wants. It may be heaped up on the mud flats to form an island, or dumped at sea. Most often it is deposited on the nearest marsh. This destroys part of the estuary's food supply. It also alters the estuary shape still more, and therefore the way that water and detritus and nutrients flow within it. In a very short time, dredging and dumping can destroy not only the baby food but also the entire nursery on which so many lives depend. It is no wonder many scientists believe that dredging and dumping cause more harm to estuary life than any other human activity.

10

When Wetland Becomes Dry Land

Clearly an arm of the sea shrinks when spoil is dumped onto its flats or marsh. It also shrinks when supports for a bridge or causeway are driven into its bottom. It shrinks, and it gains new shape. The new shape alters the flow of water and nutrients. A large ship at anchor, a barge, or even a rowboat also may change the workings of the nutrient trap. When an estuary becomes smaller, even for a short time, there is less space for animals to move about—and less food for them to eat, for fewer floating algae can grow in the shade of a ship or a bridge. And as mud flats and marshes are filled in there are of course fewer mud algae and fewer grasses to supply food.

Our arms of the sea have been slowly shrinking ever since the days when Europeans first landed in North America. This has been especially true in the estuaries offering the safest or most convenient harbors. Boston, New York, San Francisco, and many other cities grew up around estuaries, spreading inland and along the

103

shore, out onto the marshes onto flats, and even into the water itself. Before anyone quite realized what was happening, the natural shoreline had been largely erased. In its place are manmade jetties, docks, bulkheads, factories, warehouses, airports, roads, shopping centers, houses, marinas, parks, and ever more parking lots. In some places grazing land and cultivated fields replace the more productive marshes.

Watching small changes along some quiet estuary, you get an idea of how this occurs. Little by little, small changes add up. In the end they may be as damaging as any large planned development.

Until quite recent years, for example, the Great South Bay was fringed with *Spartina alterniflora*. In its shallow waters vast eelgrass jungles protected scallops and many kinds of small and young fishes. The clean sandy bottom was home to enormous numbers of oysters and clams, both hard-shelled and soft. Waterfowl and shorebirds nested there and, finding ample food, some remained all winter. Many more kinds rested and fed there during their spring and fall migrations.

Most of the time the birds were disturbed only by fishermen and clam diggers harvesting the bay. Their flat-bottomed boats moved easily through the shallow water across the flats and up the shoal creeks and rivers. Each man tied his boat to a post driven into the creek bottom. As for the creek, a few planks laid across the low marsh was enough.

But along with the rest of the human population,

the boating population too has grown enormously. And the desires of the boat owners begin to conflict with the needs of the clams and fish they want to catch—and of the gulls that follow their boats, waiting for scraps.

To start with, most creeks and rivers were dredged for the boats, and the spoil dumped onto the surrounding marshes. In place of waving spartina grass, marinas sprouted along the water's edge as did gasoline pumps, boatyards, and roads leading to nearby towns. Having solid ground to drive over, trucks come straight to the docks to pick up clams for city markets. People who want fish or clams can buy them fresh from the sea. Here and there a fish pound or a seafood restaurant has been set up. Parking lots crowd out marsh elders and even the sturdy phragmites grass.

The road is widened, bringing still more people to the water's edge. Admiring the view of water and sky, of sailboats and water skiers, they begin to dream of a house by the bay, for vacations or for year-round living. And so changes speed up.

When there is not enough land high and dry enough, the solution is obvious: fill in the marshes. Fill may be spoil from a channel. More often it is a combination of spoil and garbage and still more spoil. In many areas, marshes have been used as garbage dumps for a long time. They did not seem good for much else. Besides, it is not easy to find places to put solid wastes like old automobiles and refrigerators.

Garbage is smelly, of course, so the bay bottom is dredged to cover the mess. The sand and mud, being

105

As abandoned cars rust away at the town dump, various toxic chemicals seep into the water.

very wet, run off the dump, sloshing sediments and garbage into the bay. To keep the fill in and the tide out, a dike of earth and planks is made. Slowly the fill builds up behind it, packs down, becomes solid and dry.

At this point dredging is carefully planned. The idea is to create many small canals passing among thin fingers of land. This makes more waterfront lots, and so more money for the developer. To support these fingers, oil-soaked planks and posts are driven down into the muck. This protects the land against the sea—at least until a hurricane tears them out—and it gives each lot its own dock. And so the shoreline develops from marsh to dump to landfill to waterfront housing.

When Wetland Becomes Dry Land

Houses here, a park there, a marina and parking lot on the next creek—the changes add up. But the bay is so large, few people worry about the loss of a fish nursery. And for anyone who can afford it, a home with a dock and a bay view seems an improvement over scratchy grass and mosquitoey creeks.

But for estuary life each waterfront house, especially when constructed behind bulkheads, means a little less space for the vital marsh grasses to grow, for birds to nest in, and less food for developing fish and shrimp. In the Great South Bay alone nearly half of the marshes that existed twenty years ago are gone, buried under

Houses and docks have succeeded marsh and mud flats in this New Jersey estuary. Once buried, productive habitats are difficult to restore.

such developments. But as the bay still produces about half the United States harvest of hard clams, few people are much worried about the losses.

Yet the changes are speeding up—everywhere, not just in this one bay. For the country as a whole, eight out of every ten marshes that existed 100 years ago are gone. During the past twenty years another 700,000 acres of our most productive estuaries perished. Six states, California, Texas, Louisiana, Florida, New Jersey, and New York, account for more than 70 per cent of these losses. And still the dredging and filling continues.

As the arms of the sea shrink, their non-human populations do too. If you watch ducks and geese flocking over a Carolina or California marsh in winter, you will be impressed by the huge numbers of birds. But each year there are fewer such marshes left for the birds to flock to. As a result, they concentrate in those that remain.

Sea mammals, too, are disappearing. Manatees still crop the sea grasses in Florida lagoons, but in less than half their former numbers. Otters which once frolicked in San Francisco Bay are now rarely seen there at all. People who fish for a living and those who fish for fun are taking fewer fish for each hour spent fishing. Averaged out over five- and ten-year periods, the catches of our most important commercial fish and shellfish have declined.

Sometimes, of course, their populations decline for reasons over which people have little control. A series

Heading south, thousands of pintail ducks darken the skies above a California wild bird refuge. Even so, bird census takers report an alarming drop in the numbers of waterfowl over the past ten years.

of bad storms, an unusually cold winter, a long period of drought may kill crabs and fish as well as birds and small mammals. All too often, though, the decline can be traced to dirt in the water—sediments from dredging and filling or wastes from ships and from the land. Each boat that passes through a channel or anchors in a harbor adds some of its dirt to the water. Each house, each factory, each parking lot contributes a share. And as the human population grows, this dirt piles up faster than tides can flush it away. Indeed, pollution is growing three times faster than the population—and the world population is doubling every thirty years.

By letting the arms of the sea become so dirty, people weaken sea life. Then some natural stress may prove more than fish and crab can stand. Very often, too, pollution does more than cloud the water and cover the grasses. It may so poison the arms of the sea that they become unfit for living beings.

11

Too Many Nutrients, Not Enough Oxygen

From Cape Cod, Texas, southern California, from estuaries almost everywhere come reports of calamities: "Black ducks and herring gulls stricken" "Town Beach Closed to Swimming" "Millions of Menhaden Killed" "Ban on Mussels and Clams Continues."

All too often such events are caused by something people have done or failed to do. Sometimes the message changes. Tiny one-celled plankton organisms seem to be the principal villains. When these creatures bloom, they make the water look red. Day after day, week after week, the water glows like an endless sunset. This "red tide" kills fish, poisons clams—and birds and people.

The poison, like the red color, comes from certain kinds of dinoflagellates. The name means "terrible whip." All dinoflagellates move about by lashing the water with their threadlike whips, or *flagella*. But only a few kinds are "terrible."

These terrible, poison-producing dinoflagellates are

111

Blooms of poisonous dinoflagellates or blue-green algae cause many fish kills like this one off Sanibel Island, Florida. When any one kind of organism multiplies more rapidly than other kinds, it may so reduce oxygen or food supplies that the ecosystem becomes unbalanced.

most likely to bloom when days are long and the water warm. Often a red tide follows a period of rainy weather which lowers salinity quite suddenly and which washes in quantities of nutrients from the land. Together these events may favor a bloom of poisonous dinoflagellates.

So long as conditions are right, the bloom may continue for six weeks or more, killing many creatures. To keep on the safe side, some people avoid eating shellfish in the months spelled without an "R".

Red tides occur without help from man. But with man's help they occur more often, and their effects seem longer-lasting.

No one can do much about the weather, of course, at least not to a degree that can readily be measured. Power plants, though, do raise the temperature of estuaries. This is because they use the water to cool their equipment and then pour the water, now much warmer than before, back into the estuary. A few degrees of change in the temperature of the water may trigger a red tide and other trouble as well, especially in summer. This thermal, or heat, pollution is expected to become a more serious problem as more power plants are built. In the main, though, red tides and other such "natural" disasters result from excessive nutrient supplies. And in all cases people are to blame.

Red tides often follow dredging. Dinoflagellates thrive on the nutrients that the dredge stirs up. And, almost always, runoff from the land carries nutrients as well as sediments. When the marshes are covered over, there are no grasses to catch these nutrients as they flow toward the sea.

At the same time, wastes of all sorts are deliberately dumped into rivers and arms of the sea. Many of these wastes are harmless in themselves. They come from living or once living beings. In time they will be broken

Many paper and pulp mills like this one still discharge organic and chemical wastes directly into rivers and streams. Such wastes could readily be filtered out and the cleaned water reused in the mill.

down by bacteria and converted into nutrients that green plants can use. Streams emptying into the Penobscot River in Maine, for example, are choked with sawdust, bark, and other remains of dead trees. In some Texas estuaries, the problem is manure from cattle being fattened for market. Potato peelings from potato-

114

chip factories and grease from chicken farms are but two of the other natural, organic substances that are dumped into the water.

The dumping of some things may vary with the season. Leftovers from a fish cannery in Oregon may be a problem in fall but not in winter, for example. With sewage and household wastes, though, the dumping goes on steadily through the year. Neither tides nor bacteria have a chance to clean the water.

In about nine out of every ten estuaries, sewage is a problem. It comes from homes and factories on land, and from fishing boats and luxury liners, small pleasure craft, and giant aircraft carriers. Few watercraft have the means of cleaning their wastes before pouring them into the sea. Some towns do treat sewage and garbage and sell the end product as fertilizer and mulch for crops. But those towns are exceptions. Most fertilize rivers and arms of the sea instead. (In a way, this means estuaries are fertilized twice. When chemical fertilizers are used on land, they seep out of the soil and quickly end up in the water.)

Neither chemical fertilizers nor body wastes are poisonous in the way that oil and DDT are. But because they favor the growth of sea plants—and some kinds more than others—they end up harming the estuary.

Some plankton organisms thrive on phosphates. These may come from duck droppings, fertilizers, detergents, or from the mining of phosphate rock. When supplies of phosphates are abundant, green flagellates grow rapidly, crowding out diatoms. But clams and

115

oysters cannot digest green flagellates as easily as diatoms. Stuffed with the wrong sort of plankton, they may grow slowly or even starve.

Some large seaweeds also may grow too rapidly. Scallops whose shells are covered thickly with *Codium*, for example, may be unable to move. A thick mat of *Enteromorpha* on the bottom holds the sun's heat and makes the sand fatally warm for animals living within it.

Like dead spartina, organic wastes must be decayed before their nutrients are released. It is in the process of breaking down that these wastes most injure estuary life. For the decay bacteria consume oxygen, and sometimes this may leave little oxygen for other living beings.

Though sea plants, large and microscopic, produce oxygen, most is "lost" into the air, becoming part of the air we breathe. The sea picks up the oxygen its creatures use when waves break or winds ripple the surface, when tides and rivers meet and mix the air and water. In calm weather the wind does little mixing, and sometimes the water hardly moves at all. In summer, especially, when oxygen tends to "cook" out of water into air, some bays become very stagnant indeed. This happens frequently in the Laguna Madre and other shallow lagoons where people have greatly altered the natural movements of the water.

Yet it is at such times that active creatures like fish want and use more oxygen. One summer about 15,000,000 menhaden were lured into Escambia Bay, Florida, by a luxuriant plankton bloom. There were so many fish that they quickly exhausted what little oxygen was available. The fish died, thereby increasing the food supply for the bacteria and so further depleting oxygen supplies.

When scientists study the health of a body of water, they take samples of living plants and animals. They also weigh the amount of dead organic material. In this way they can estimate the amount of oxygen that bacteria will use while breaking it down. This provides a measure of an estuary's health known as the biochemical oxygen demand, or BOD. When the demand for oxygen exceeds the available supply, the ecosystem is unbalanced. Unless more oxygen somehow becomes dissolved in the water, entire food webs may collapse.

In the absence of oxygen, most sea bacteria die. Then the process of decay is taken over by other kinds that can live without oxygen. However, these bacteria give off hydrogen sulfide, a gas that smells like rotten eggs and is poisonous to many animals. By this time, though, there are few animals left to poison.

Sometimes an arm of the sea smells bad because of decaying sewage, and yet, because oxygen levels are adequate, remains home for worms and clams and fish. All the same such an estuary may be unhealthy because sewage contains disease germs that can infect birds and mammals, including people. To protect people—if not the other animals—most states require that water be tested at regular intervals. Most often such tests are for coliform bacteria, which, though not harmful in themselves, indicate the presence of sewage and

117

so of harmful organisms. As coliform counts rise, public health officials close the infected water to shellfishing, to swimming if necessary, and in extreme cases to fishing as well. As a result of such tests, shellfishing is banned in one third of all our estuaries. More such areas are closed each year.

Sometimes estuaries are closed because poisonous substances have been dumped into the water. Under such conditions not even dinoflagellates can flourish. As someone has written, pollution is the most accurate term to describe man's effect on his surroundings.

12

A Witch's Brew

Banana skin canoes and grapefruit rowboats drift against buoys of soda cans and bleach jugs. Tides move them to shore and whirl them away again. These fleets of garbage are ugly and even dangerous. Fish die when their intestines become clogged with polystyrene. A shark can starve to death with a beer can plugging its throat. A goose cannot swallow if it gets its neck caught in a plastic ring. And sea turtles suffocate under sheets of plastic.

Far more dangerous to sea life, however, is the poisonous litter that one way or another is dumped into the arms of the sea. Poisons are poured over estuaries deliberately, as when planes spray mosquitoes and flies. But they also come from afar upland, drifting through the air in tiny droplets. They trickle down through the ground with rainwater. They flow in torrents down a river. The tide may flush the poisons out to sea, but even there the damage goes on. Toxic, or poisonous, litter takes a long time to disappear.

119

An eighth-grader holds a Canada goose found dead near Long Island
Sound with part of a plastic six-pack carrier stuck in its throat.

Pesticides from farms and forests, along with toxic wastes from factories and mines, form much of this deadly litter. Oil, which will be discussed in the next chapter, accounts for the rest.

The word "pesticide" means pest *killer*. In a sense, a flyswatter fits that definition. With it you may kill all the flies in your house. And flies, almost everyone would agree, are pests. With a chemical pesticide, though, you may kill all the flies in the neighborhood—at least for a time.

With some such hopes people spray cropland, orchards, forests, lawns, rose gardens, and even thickets of wildflowers by the roadsides. For a pest may be a weed that competes for space and nutrients with plants that people want. More often the pest is an insect that feeds on these plants. It may also be a fungus disease that weakens or kills them.

By combining chemical substances in new ways, chemists have developed ten hundred poisons, each designed to do a particular job. But a poison that kills one living being can kill others, and it usually does. So blue-claw crabs and mullet become victims along with the pest.

Some pesticides, such as the weedkillers 2, 4, 5-T and 2, 4-D, can damage unborn mammals including humans. Others act more immediately. Parathion, for example, is so poisonous that a few drops on your hand will kill you. It is hard to believe that such a tiny amount of anything can be lethal. Perhaps that is why people tend to be careless in using these poisons.

121

However, the pesticides known as chlorinated hydrocarbons are probably the most dangerous of all. This is because they are so widely used and so long-lasting. DDT is the most familiar example. Along with benzene hexachloride, toxaphene and endrin, it has now been banned for most purposes. Others still in use include dieldrin, heptachlor, chlordane, and lindane.

These products are sometimes called "hard" pesticides because they break down so slowly. DDT, for example, decays into DDD and DDE, but these compounds are almost as poisonous as their "mother." Fifty years may pass before the last trace disappears. About one quarter of the hard pesticides ever produced probably still exist, drifting about in the sea. And as more poison is sprayed, it builds up in soil, in marshes and mud flats, and in the water. In some arms of the sea, DDT and its daughters can be measured not in drops, but in pounds per acre though no one would ever dream of applying such a dose at one time. And so long as it lasts, this poison will go on harming living beings.

The poison has both immediate and long-lasting effects. If a marsh is sprayed for mosquitoes, the pests do die. So do dragonflies and damselflies that eat them and the killifish that pursue mosquito larvae across the low marsh. So do fiddler crabs lurking in their burrows, young blue claws and shrimp feeding in the shallows. So do the copepods, those tiny links in so many food chains.

In a short time millions of animals may be dead.

The pilots of the spray planes do not see what happens as the spray falls. And if the victims are not animals that people eat, no one else much notices either. And even if people do notice, they do not always want to stop spraying. For example, dieldrin was sprayed one year along some Florida lagoons. Sandflies feeding on dead seaweeds had gotten to be a nuisance to sunbathers. The dieldrin killed the flies, and it killed fish. In the end over 25 tons of fish, representing 30 species, had to be shoveled off the beaches. Even so, the next year when the sandflies appeared town officials planned to spray again.

Dieldrin and DDT kill mosquitoes and sandflies and most other insects, whether harmful to people and their crops or not. They also kill shrimp, crab, copepods and other crustaceans. Eggs and larvae succumb even more quickly than fully grown individuals. Because crustaceans are closely related to insects, this is not too surprising. Fish, which are not related to insects, are even more sensitive to the poison. And though insects build up immunity to it, fish never do.

To learn more about how the chlorinated hydrocarbons affect fish, scientists at the University of Miami set up tanks containing 6 parts of dieldrin to a billion parts of water—about the same concentration you might find in water a few days after spraying. (If you were foolish enough to add 6 drops of dieldrin to water in a swimming pool 15 by 30 feet and about 5 feet deep, you would have a similar solution.)

The scientists placed small fish—sailfin mollies and

sheepshead minnows—in these tanks. Within a few minutes they examined the gills of the fish. They found concentrations of dieldrin reached from 8,000 to 10,000 parts per billion.

As the fish move water over their gills, they soak up poison. In summer when marshes and beaches are most likely to be sprayed, water is warm and dissolved oxygen low. Fish work hard to get what oxygen there is. This means they take in pesticides more rapidly than ever. They do this very efficiently indeed. When the water in the test tanks was analyzed forty-eight hours later, it contained less than 0.01 parts per billion or 1 part per trillion. The water was almost "clean." But the fish were now "dirty."

Surveying estuaries in southeastern Florida, these scientists found that all the water and most of the fish contained some DDT, dieldrin or both. Because chlorinated hydrocarbons do not occur naturally, living beings have not developed the ability to excrete them as they have for most wastes. The poison is taken in and stored in the fatty tissues of their bodies. If the amounts remain small—and each species can tolerate a little—the poison appears not to harm them. In time of stress, however, even a small amount proves fatal.

When a fish migrates, for example, it stops feeding and begins to draw on its fat reserve. This may release the poison suddenly in a dose big enough to kill the fish.

The stored poison also lessens the fish's chances of survival in other ways. As it builds up, it affects the

124

nervous system, and so alters the animal's behavior. A flounder may become too slow and clumsy to catch sand shrimp. It may fail to conceal itself at low tide, becoming an easy meal for an osprey—in which case the poison is passed on to the bird. And the more poisoned fish the osprey eats, the more its own behavior may be altered.

As the poison moves through a food web, it builds up and becomes magnified in a most unhealthy way. Studying pesticide residues in a marsh that is now part of the Wertheim National Wildlife Refuge in New York, scientists analyzed marsh mud, bay bottom, water, and plant and animal life. In plankton samples, DDT levels reached about 0.04 parts per million. In a ring-billed gull, at the other end of the food chain, the concentration was 75 parts per million. In an osprey, a fish hawk that breeds in the area, DDT concentrations were 300,000 times higher than those in their fishing waters.

If one or two birds were this "dirty," no one would worry too much. But in wildlife refuges around the country the stories are much the same. Populations of ospreys, eagles, egrets, ibises, ducks, terns, and gulls are declining as more adult birds die each year than young ones survive to replace them. Several species appear close to extinction. The brown pelican is an example.

This ungainly-looking bird nests on islands along the Gulf of Mexico and southern California coasts. But in a recent year park rangers in the Channel Islands

Normal-sized tern's egg (foreground) has been set next to two abnormally small and one abnormally large egg. Some eggs found at Great Gull Island, New York, had no shells at all.

National Monument of California noted that among 540 pairs making nests, only four pairs produced live offspring.

Walking over the rocky islands whitened by the droppings from generations of birds, the rangers gathered the eggs that failed to hatch. Many eggs had shells so thin that they had broken when the parents sat on them. Some eggs appeared to have had no shells at all. When the contents of the eggs were analyzed, scientists found pesticide residues of up to 1,800 parts per million.

No one had sprayed marshes off the Channel Islands, for there are no marshes. Nor had chemical factories flushed out tanks nearby, for there are no such factories in that area. Rather the pesticides seemed to be coming from farms, vineyards, and orchards near the coast. And the fish upon which the pelicans feed had cleaned the water well, storing the poison in their flesh and so passing it on to the pelicans.

Pesticides build up in living tissue. They also build up and are concentrated in some areas by physical forces such as winds and tides. And these areas are often where pelicans and other birds feed.

If you ever sail on a sound or lagoon, you are sure to watch the wind. As it fills your sail, you can see it ruffle the water. But here and there you can see calm patches. No one has spread any fish oil to calm the water. The slicks seem instead to be caused by waves building up along the interface between waters of differing salinities or temperatures. The slicks may also be caused by the wind itself, though no one knows precisely how.

As the two masses of water meet, the nutrients suspended in them are pressed together, forming a thick film. (If there is fuel oil in the water, it may be pressed into thick lumps of tar.) If you watch the slick closely, you will observe that diving ducks and other birds often float along with the slicks. Drawing on the abundant nutrients, plant plankton thrive. So do animal plankton, and so on up the food chain to the birds themselves.

Unfortunately, pesticides are also compressed into these slicks. In some way too the poisons may bubble up from the bottom, keeping up the supply. If oil is present, it tends to hold the poisons much as a magnet hold iron. When scientists tested the water in slicks in Biscayne Bay in Florida, they found that concentrations of pesticides were 10,000 times greater than they were even a few inches lower down.

Analyzing such slicks, scientists have found traces of many toxic substances, including lead, copper, and other heavy metals along with polychlorinated biphenyls, or PCB's. Related chemically to the chlorinated hydrocarbons, the PCB's are widely used in making plastics, paints, and electrical equipment. They are valued by manufacturers for the very reason they are so dangerous in the sea—they last a long time, perhaps 100 times longer than DDT. And for all that time they will remain extremely poisonous.

Alerted to the dangers, some manufacturers are becoming more careful in disposing of factory wastes. Many scientists believe that PCB's may be reaching the sea mainly from the air. Let us say, for example, that you have a badly scratched phonograph record or an empty plastic shampoo container. Being tough and strong, it does not break if you drop it or step on it. If you burn it, it seems to disappear, but only "seems." For then PCB particles move into the air and eventually fall out over water. There, like DDT, they are taken in by living organisms and stored in their body tissues.

128

The heavy metals build up in food chains in much the same way. Not long ago public health officials condemned catches of tuna and swordfish containing so much mercury that they were unsafe for people to eat. (For that matter, people are unfit for human con-

Even if this embryo tern had succeeded in hatching, its crossed bill would have prevented it from feeding. Other fatal defects are appearing in chicks on refuges from Massachusetts to Florida. Scientists blame high levels of PCB's, found in birds' fatty tissues.

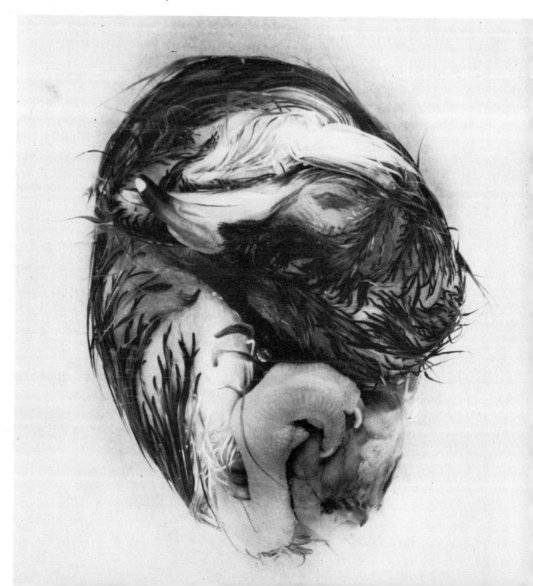

sumption.) If the fishes had lived long enough, they would eventually have secreted the mercury. For mercury and other heavy metals occur naturally in rocks from which they are carved out by wind and weather and washed into estuaries. Sea creatures have had millions of years to become adjusted to such tiny amounts. So though a fish takes in lead or mercury and stores it, it can also get rid of it before it causes any harm.

However, as people mine the earth and use its metals in their factories and on their farms, the quantities in the sea are increasing rapidly. Living beings are taking in the metals faster than they can get rid of them.

In above-normal concentrations, heavy metals begin to interfere with life processes. They tend, for example, to affect gill tissue and blood vessels, thus reducing a fish's ability to absorb oxygen. Such an impairment can prove fatal when little oxygen is available in the water.

Like vast witch's caldrons, the arms of the sea receive about 500,000 natural and unnatural substances each year. Several hundred of these are known to be dangerous to sea life, and more are being created all the time. Seldom if ever are new chemicals tested on water animals before being allowed to flow into waste pipes or rivers. And of course pesticides are mainly tested on the original pest.

"Cooking" together in the sunlight or in heated water from a power plant, stirred about by currents and tides, these substances act and react with one another in ways

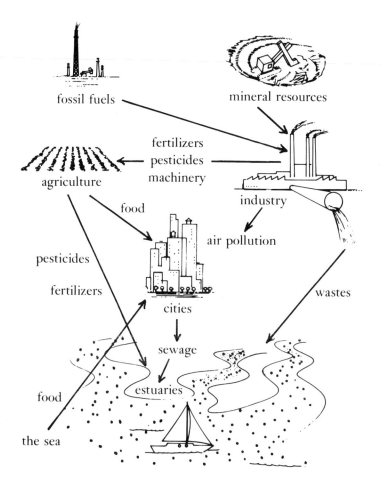

Relation between people, their activities, and the sea.

that are little understood. Chemicals from a factory react with chemicals from a farm, producing new compounds which may be more harmful than either substance alone. Nickel, for example, becomes ten times more poisonous in combination with copper.

Because many of the substances now pouring into estuaries are so new, no one can predict how poisonous this witch's brew may become. And with millions of barrels of oil for seasoning, the results are frightful to think about.

131

13

Oil Troubles the Waters

After walking along a beach you often come home with small "pancakes" of tar stuck to your feet. If the estuary has a harbor near a large city, you probably always come home that way. For the tar is oil that was spilled into the sea and has drifted ashore.

This slimy gooey stuff makes the water and the beach dirty. It makes your feet and clothing dirty too. Worse still, it makes water plants and animals dirty. And if it coats their leaves or skins or gills, it kills them.

Though birds are not the only victims, they are usually the most visible ones, especially after barge or tanker accidents or leaks from offshore oil wells. Most of all, the spilled oil endangers ducks, grebes, and other seabirds that swim about on the water. To feed or to escape enemies, such birds dive under the water. Because of this habit they quickly become soaked with any oil that may be in the water. When their wings and bodies are heavy with oil, they are unable to swim, unable to fly. Then they may drown or starve. Or

132

A common eider duck is dying, its body soaked with oil spilled off Cape Cod.

they may die of exposure since oil, displacing air among their feathers, destroys their insulation against cold. Even a small blotch of oil on the skin may lower a bird's temperature to a fatal degree.

One of the best-known oil-drilling accidents occurred in the Santa Barbara Channel off California. Each day for almost two weeks 21,000 gallons of oil gushed from the ocean floor, covering sea and shore for miles around with oil and toxic drilling muds. As a result of this uncontrollable leak, or blowout, about a third of all the birds that lived or wintered in that area were killed. Volunteers cleaned many birds, but could save very few. The birds had swallowed too much oil in trying to preen their own feathers. Though the oil did not kill them outright, it lowered their ability to resist disease. Thus many cleaned birds died from quite ordinary infections.

Everyone hears about big blowouts like the ones at Santa Barbara, Cook Inlet, and Main Block Pass off Louisiana. Many people see wrecked tankers like the *Ocean Eagle* and the *Torrey Canyon*. For it is when tankers are close to shore that they most often collide, go aground, or even capsize. And refineries onshore sometimes suffer leaks, fires, and explosions that can be smelled as well as seen or heard.

Almost unnoticed, though, are the smaller accidents of everyday. In one year without a single major disaster, almost nine thousand spills were recorded by the United States Coast Guard, the agency responsible for preventing or cleaning up harmful discharges into our navigable waters. Although most of these spills involve less than one thousand gallons of oil, the total reaches eight to nine million gallons each year. (There are many crude oils and oil products, each suited to a particular purpose. Despite their physical differences, they have similar chemical and biological effects. So for convenience the term "oil" here stands for all such substances

Oil flows from underneath drilling platform (top right) toward the line of barges and booms set out to slow the spread of oil.

from "light" gasoline and kerosene to "heavy" fuel and diesel oils.)

Accidents, small or catastrophic, account for less than a third of all the oil spilled into rivers, estuaries, and the sea. The rest, amounting each year to more than three million metric tons, and possibly twice or three times that, comes from automobile and boat engines and from factories. When you think that there is one car for every two people in the United States, not counting buses, trucks, and farm machinery, you can readily imagine how the oil mounts up. When motor oil is changed in a car, for example, the old oil is usually dumped down a service station drain or flushed into a gutter. Either way it flows into sewers—and on into the sea. Each year oil in Los Angeles sewage alone equals or exceeds the amount that gushed into the sea during the first ten days of the Santa Barbara blowout.

A detectable, though perhaps unmeasurable, share comes through the air as tiny particles of unburned heating fuel, from car exhausts, from motor boats, from jet planes. Also falling out of the air into the sea come lead and other harmful pollutants.

Drop by drop, gallon by gallon, these "spills" add up. Like many small physical changes along the shore, they end up causing more damage than any newsmaking disaster.

Compared to the mercury compounds, PCB's and hard pesticides, all this oil seems harmless. It disappears from the water by evaporating into the air, by dissolving, and by decay. But when oil is spilled close to shore, it has very little time to disappear.

Let us imagine what happens when fishing boats, one by one, pump their oily bilges into a marina, spreading a lovely rainbow around them. Oil, as everyone knows, floats on water. As it floats, oil bathes plankton in its poisonous vapors. Some plankton organisms die,

A sharp increase in the number of pleasure boats such as these at a Florida marina means increased pollution of several kinds. Two of the most serious are water pollution from engine oils and air pollution from partial combustion.

while others store the oil as they do DDT. Winds and waves spread the oil over the surface. Propellers and oars stir it about. So the poison covers an even wider area.

Much diluted now, it does not kill living creatures when they swallow it. But it builds up in living tissues. Passed along a food chain, it may give a fish or clam an oily taste, which may lead to the condemning of an entire catch. More serious, it may cause cancer and other growths in fish. And the cancer-causing substance can be passed along the food chain to people.

Oil floats, but it also moves downward. If the water is clear, you can see oil shimmering like a veil between the boats. This veil kills mollusk larvae, fish eggs, young fish fry, and even adult fish sometimes.

The heavier fractions, or parts, of the oil settle to the bottom. Like a great blanket, they smother oysters and other animals that cannot move away. If the blanket is thin enough, such animals may survive, but most likely their flesh will become too tainted to eat.

Becoming churned up and mixed with bottom sediments, the oil stays there, killing or tainting bottom life. If waves sweep the oily sediments ashore, the oil may then poison the roots and stems of the vital marsh grasses. It may make the marsh mud unfit for any life.

Once mixed with and buried under marsh mud and bottom sediment, oil cannot evaporate. And it cannot decay. For the kinds of sea bacteria that break down oil need light and oxygen—conditions lacking in the mud. Water temperatures, too, must be just right. If the water is cold and deep, as it is in Cook Inlet or Puget Sound, bacteria feed and grow very slowly.

In the Gulf of Mexico, the water may be warm enough, but oxygen levels may be too low. Bacteria consume an astonishing amount of oxygen in breaking down one gallon of oil. In experiments at one oil company they were found to use all the oxygen in 320,000 gallons of water. If an estuary is warm and shallow, and if the biochemical oxygen demand is already high, oil-decaying bacteria may be unable to finish off the oil. And the part that remains is usually the most poisonous part. For these bacteria feed on the least poisonous part first. Moreover, wastes from the oil-decaying bacteria may themselves be harmful. Finally, bacteria seem unable to make a dent in those horrid tar balls.

Bacteria cannot reach oil once it enters the food chain. Then instead of disappearing, the poisonous fractions become biologically magnified. Passed through the food web, oil disappears only when an organism dies and is decayed by bacteria.

Scientists in one oil company research laboratory estimate that proportions of oil to water are already about 6 parts per billion in major shipping lanes. They are probably higher in some arms of the sea. At these levels they are known to interfere with the response of animals to their surroundings. Lobsters, for example, are attracted to oily water. Somehow they prefer its odor to that of their normal food. In the case of a spill, this preference may mean that the lobsters get smothered by the oil. At other times they may simply starve.

Oil prevents animals from finding food and from detecting enemies. It may keep some from finding the right spawning areas. For example, oil seems to block the sense of smell in salmon. Unable to smell home waters, a fish may exhaust itself trying to find the proper stream or spawn in the wrong sort of place. Then its eggs may be washed away or eaten before they can hatch.

Probably oil has leaked into the sea ever since the first deposits were formed, and to some degree plants and animals living near oozy places have become adjusted to the oil. Spilled oil does not seem to harm surf grass or certain kinds of worms. But of course concentrations of oil keep increasing, and no one knows how the increase may affect even such oil-tolerant species.

Oil deposits on land are fast being used up. This means more oil will have to be drawn from under the sea—in time, about one third of all we use. Accidents in exploring, in drilling, and in moving it to shore will become more frequent. At the same time larger and larger tankers will bring oil from other countries. The new crude-oil carriers can hold 300,000 tons. Others are being planned to take 1,000,000 tons. Such supertankers will be better equipped than small ones to clean up accidents, but each accident may prove far more disastrous than any in the past.

One gigantic spill or thousands of small ones can destroy mile upon mile of healthy estuaries, and of beaches people enjoy. One way or another, human activities conflict with the life processes of fish and wildlife.

We do want seafood and clean beaches. Yet we also want oil to power our machines and to warm our houses. Somehow people must find a way of balancing their conflicting desires. Some first small steps are being taken, but many more are necessary if the arms of the sea are to survive.

140

14

In the Future

Rocked by the turning earth, warmed by the sun, refreshed by rivers and surging sea, the estuaries shelter sea life, seen and unseen. Tall grasses and tiny seaweeds nourish sea worm and shrimp, snail, clam, minnow, and eel. Small fish feed big fish, merganser, and loon. And many such creatures feed people.

Still, people tend to forget how important estuaries are since most of the seafood we eat is caught *outside* them. But except for tuna and cod, most shellfish and finfish grow and develop *inside* them. This is true even with menhaden and other species that spawn in the sea. It is in the estuaries that they grow big enough to be caught later.

As the sea nurseries shrink and become dirty, fish and shellfish populations too are shrinking and becoming dirty, sometimes too dirty to be eaten. At the same time people from many nations fish the seas more hungrily than ever. The human populations of the world are growing, and many depend on seafood for much

Like other Indians of the northwest coast, Quileutes harvest salmon, setting nets from boats like these seiners anchored at a reservation village. Until rivers were cut off by huge dams and destroyed by pollution, salmon swarmed upstream in five or more major runs each year, and the Indians prospered.

of their animal protein, if not all of it. Even in the United States this may be so indirectly, for tons of menhaden and other fish become meal for poultry, cattle, and chicken.

Under pressure from human activities on sea and on land, many fish and shellfish appear headed for extinction. This includes haddock, cod, fluke, and lobster. To stop the decline and indeed to increase the supply, people of the fishing nations must agree on rules limiting the size of their catches. They also need better rules for using their shorelines and for disposing of their wastes. They need better rules—and they need to keep them better.

142

To make good rules, though, we need to know more about the sea and its life. Surprisingly, the sea which people have fished for so long is still largely unknown, unexplored, and the habits of its creatures more mysterious than the moon. This is true even for salmon, which have probably been studied more than most other sea animals.

Salmon have been tagged and followed on their journeys downriver as young fry, during their great voyages through the sea—some sockeye travel 10,000 miles in two or three years—and during their homing migrations. In various experiments scientists have determined that while salmon use sun or moon as a compass, chemical clues, such as changes in salt, are more important

Park rangers in airboats patrol the marshes of the Everglades to enforce rules protecting plants and wildlife.

in guiding them home. But they do not know how the fish navigate in cloudy weather or which chemical substances are most useful.

And no one knows how salmon time their arrival in home waters so precisely. Fishermen know they can expect salmon of a particular species to arrive within a few days of that species' return the previous year. It seems that the fish are somehow born knowing the time when river flow, water temperature, and dissolved oxygen levels will most favor their passage upriver. But if people understood such things better, they might be able to guide migrating salmon toward streams unspoiled by dams and power plants. They might also be able to "farm" the fish more successfully.

People need to know more about the feeding habits and growth rates of fish. As it is, when you catch a small flounder, say, you have no reliable way of knowing how old it is. You may guess from its size that it is not fully grown, has not yet produced its own kind. To some extent commercial fishermen too are guessing when they decide which fish to keep and which to throw back into the sea. Even if a fish is fully developed, there is often little way of knowing whether or not it has had a chance to spawn. With accurate information about each species, fishermen could select nets and hooks to catch only mature fish. To make sure that such fish had been able to spawn at least once, certain seasons might be closed for fishing.

With underwater laboratories and other modern equipment, such studies are becoming possible. Unfortunately, human activities are changing the sea and its arms so rapidly that some studies may prove impossible. For example, no one knew much about animal and plant populations living at various seasons in the Santa Barbara Channel before the blowouts. Without such basic information it was difficult to learn the damage or to correct it. Thus though marine scientists may have the necessary tools, they may be faced only with a series of "afters" for study.

For this reason some people have proposed that five unspoiled estuaries be set aside for intensive study of the "befores," one in the cold waters of Alaska, another in Maine, and one each in the warmer waters of the Atlantic and Pacific oceans and the Gulf of Mexico. By studying life in these preserves over long periods of time, scientists would gain detailed information about each species and develop some basis for understanding changes in other, similar estuaries.

But of course such preserves cannot be cut off from the sea. Lethal PCB's and other pollutants are carried by sea currents and winds far from the places where they were "spilled." So until people know more about sea life and how their activities may affect it, a wiser course is to protect all the remaining estuaries.

Many town, state, and federal officials already recognize—at least in words—that the arms of the sea are the most valuable of our remaining natural resources. In California, for example, a Coastal Zone Conservation Commission is drawing up plans to rescue the coastline and its estuaries from further development. Meanwhile

145

almost all dredging and filling is prohibited. If someone attempts to dump or dredge without a permit, individual citizens can report the action, knowing it will be stopped. This watchdog role is very important in enforcing the law and may become part of coastal protection plans in other states.

Of course some dredging will always be necessary to keep channels open to ships. To lessen the need for such work, the Army Corps of Engineers, which is responsible for maintaining our waterways, proposes to create islands or floating platforms offshore. There supertankers could unload their oil directly into pipelines buried beneath the sea floor. This system would reduce the chance of oil spills in the nursery areas. It would mean too that some present dock areas could become parks, marinas, and even beaches.

Proposals for locating nuclear power plants offshore are also being studied. Though thermal pollution may cause less damage there than in the nurseries, getting rid of radioactive wastes will still be a problem. And as yet no one knows how the construction and the very presence of such structures will affect sea life.

With better knowledge of physical forces such as tides and currents, people may plan inshore channels and even power plants far more successfully than in the past. Such channels may actually improve water circulation within estuaries and require dredging out less often. And if all such work is done in the winter, sediments can settle before plankton blooms in the spring and before most animals spawn.

146

A large-scale model of the Columbia River mouth, looking across entrance channel from Washington toward Oregon, with Pacific Ocean to the right. With such models the Army Corps of Engineers and independent research groups can study tides and tidal currents (produced here by generators in the "ocean"). They can observe how wastes and sediments are deposited or swept away. Because the model uses both fresh and salt water, they can learn more about the actual patterns of circulation within an estuary.

As a rule, once a marsh or mud flat is destroyed the damage cannot be repaired. However, so long as dredging soil is not badly polluted, it may be used to create new marshes. Public efforts in Jamaica Bay in New York City and in San Diego Bay show that this is possible.

About twenty years ago such spoil was used to dike

out part of the bay and to create a separate body of fresh water. Its shores have been planted to many kinds of trees, shrubs and grasses, creating an admirable wild-life refuge and sanctuary which attracts thousands of migrating and non-migrating birds—and thousands of bird watchers. In San Diego a "people refuge" was planned instead with miles of beaches, boat launching ramps, and other tourist facilities. Since sewage no longer flows into the bay, fish and other wildlife too are benefiting from the clean water.

Even as estuaries are restored, people must work hard to keep their wastes out of the water. This is as true for people far inland as for people in boats on the sea. After all, wastes, like weeds, are simply things that appear where you do not want them. Often, like weeds, they have a use that is not obvious at first glance. Old glass, for example, can be ground up fine and used in place of sand in building roads and houses. And if glass is used, sand will not have to be dredged from an estuary.

One New Jersey oil company is re-refining dirty motor oil. The cleaned oil can be used by motorists like any new oil, and much of the "dirt"—chemicals and metals—can be put to good use. Some solid wastes can be turned into fuel or burned to produce steam for power plants. Sewage, of course, can be treated and returned to the soil as fertilizer.

Some farmers already, by planting and cultivating crops more scientifically, find they have less need for expensive pesticides. They let living controls, such as ladybird beetles and parasitic wasps, gobble up harmful insects—a practice home gardeners too can follow. And when they need pesticides, they use a product that degrades rapidly and kills as few non-target organisms as possible.

In such ways people may some day succeed in protecting the arms of the sea from further damage. Even then the seafood harvest will probably not be adequate for the growing world population. To increase this harvest, many people believe that estuaries must be farmed, much as inland lakes and ponds have been in other countries. China, for example, raises millions of pounds of freshwater fish in well-managed ponds.

In the United States sea farming is still in an experimental stage. For many years, of course, fish hatcheries have operated on both east and west coasts. Because salmon and other fishes have been cut off from their home streams by dams and pollution, hatcheries provide a way—often the only way—to maintain their populations. As salmon approach their home waters, they are caught and stripped of eggs and milt. Placed in tanks where conditions are carefully controlled, a large number of eggs and young survive. Technicians feed and tend the young fish for two years or more. At last they release them into the sea where the fish complete their development.

If scientists knew exactly which substances a salmon responds to and follows home, sea farmers might use these substances to attract fish to their farms. By using them in hatchery tanks, the farmer could "teach" fish

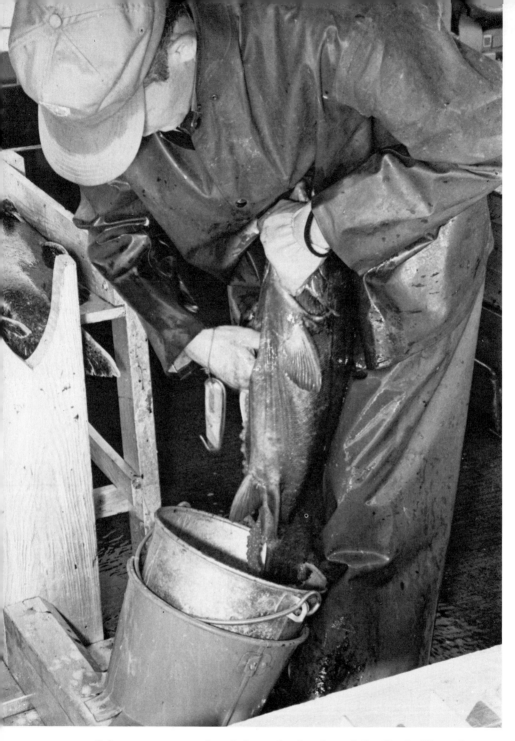

Salmon eggs are stripped from the female and fertilized. Then they are placed in trays where they grow and develop in predator-free surroundings.

Oysters live attached to empty oyster shells which form vast beds across the bottom of some estuaries. By hanging strings of shells from rafts, researcher for Oxford (Maryland) Biological Laboratory encourages oyster larvae to settle in the plankton-rich upper waters of Chesapeake Bay.

to return to the farm rather than to their ancestral stream.

Some kinds of fish may be kept in captivity throughout their lives. Because those fish grow faster than wild fish, scientists hope in time to breed new stocks that will grow even faster. Some predict that protein yields per acre of estuary may be 500 pounds or more each year. This is about six times the weight of fish that can be taken from a healthy, unfarmed estuary and about 25 times that of cattle raised on an acre of dry land.

Shellfish farms promise even higher yields of protein.

151

In Angleton, Texas, white shrimp are being raised on artificial feed in ponds where salinity and other conditions are controlled. Experimenters believe that they can harvest 2000 pounds of shrimp per acre, not just once but from three to five times a year. At Woods Hole, Massachusetts, a biologist has been growing algae on partly treated sewage. The algae are then fed to mollusks. This system has the double advantage of recycling the sewage and of producing about 20,000 pounds of seafood per acre each year.

In the future, perhaps most of the seafood we eat will be "farmed" in the arms of the sea. When and if this happens, an estuary will perhaps seem no more mysterious than a barnyard. A loss of mystery is a very real loss. Yet balanced against this will be the gain in knowledge and understanding of the estuary ecosystem. And with such understanding surely we shall appreciate it more.

Thoughtful management of estuaries and their life means rules, of course, just where we expect to find some relief from all the rules that bind together human society. Yet without rules, our vital and productive estuaries—and the sea itself—will not survive. In the end, new satisfactions may come in preserving these last frontiers—openings through which crowded land dwellers can glimpse the freedom and wildness of the untamed sea.

Books for Further Reading

Marston Bates, *The Forest and the Sea*. New York: Random House, Inc., 1960. Also available in paperback.

Greg M. Cailliet and others, *Everyman's Guide to Ecological Living*. New York: The Macmillan Company, 1971. Also available in paperback.

Rachel Carson, *The Edge of the Sea*. Boston: Houghton Mifflin Company, 1955. Also available in paperback.

Elizabeth Clemons, *Waves, Tides and Currents*. New York: Alfred A. Knopf, 1967

Lois and Louis Darling, *A Place in the Sun: Ecology and the Living World*. New York: William Morrow & Company, Inc., 1968. Excellent diagrams illustrate basic principles of ecology.

Environmental Protection Agency, *Don't Leave It All to the Experts: The Citizen's Role in Environmental Decision Making*. Washington, D.C.: U.S. Government Printing Office, 1972. Also available in paperback.

William A. Niering, *The Life of the Marsh*. New York: McGraw-Hill Book Company, Inc., 1967

Laurence Pringle, *Ecology: Science of Survival*. New York: The Macmillan Company, 1971

Laurence Pringle, *This Is a River: Exploring an Ecosystem*. New York: The Macmillan Company, 1972

John and Mildred Teal, *The Life and Death of the Salt Marsh*. Boston: Little, Brown & Company, 1969. Also available in paperback.

155

Index

Italics indicate illustration